Twenty Mock Mathcounts

http://www.mymathcounts.com/index.php

ACKNOWLEDGEMENTS

We would like to thank the following math contests:

The Mathcounts Competitions, the nation's premier middle school math enrichment, coaching, and competition program. Some of the mock tests are modified/inspired from their problems.

Junior High Math Comtest, a math competition very similar in format and timing to Mathcounts for middle school students. Some of the mock tests are modified/inspired from their tests.

We would like to mention that even some problems are modified/inspired from Mathcounts and JHMC, no single problem is repeated from their tests. Some of the problems are our own. All the solutions are our own. So if you find any mistakes, it will be on us, not on Mathcounts or JHMC.

Please contact us at mymahcounts@gmail.com for suggestions, corrections, or clarifications.

Copyright © 2013, 2014 by mymathcounts.com. All rights reserved. Printed in the United States of America. Reproduction of any portion of this book without the written permission of the authors is strictly prohibited, except as may be expressly permitted by the U.S. Copyright Act.

ISBN-13: 978-1482600803
ISBN-10: 1482600803

TABLE OF CONTENTS

1. Mathcounts Target Round Test 1 and solutions … 1

2. Mathcounts Target Round Test 2 and solutions … 10

3. Mathcounts Target Round Test 3 and solutions … 18

4. Mathcounts Target Round Test 4 and solutions … 27

5. Mathcounts Target Round Test 5 and solutions … 36

6. Mathcounts Target Round Test 6 and solutions … 45

7. Mathcounts Target Round Test 7 and solutions … 54

8. Mathcounts Target Round Test 8 and solutions … 63

9. Mathcounts Target Round Test 9 and solutions … 71

10. Mathcounts Target Round Test 10 and solutions … 79

11. Mathcounts Target Round Test 11 and solutions … 89

12. Mathcounts Target Round Test 12 and solutions … 99

13. Mathcounts Target Round Test 13 and solutions … 108

14. Mathcounts Target Round Test 14 and solutions … 115

15. Mathcounts Target Round Test 15 and solutions … 124

16. Mathcounts Target Round Test 16 and solutions … 134

17. Mathcounts Target Round Test 17 and solutions … 142

18. Mathcounts Target Round Test 18 and solutions … 151

19. Mathcounts Target Round Test 19 and solutions … 160

20. Mathcounts Target Round Test 20 and solutions … 171

Index … 180

This page is intentionally left blank.

Twenty Mathcounts Target Round Tests Test 1

MATHCOUNTS

■ Mock Competition One ■

Target Round

Name _____

State _____

DO NOT BEGIN UNTIL YOU ARE INSTRUCTED TO DO SO.

This section of the competition consists of eight problems, which will be presented in pairs. Work on one pair of problems will be completed and answers will be collected before the next pair is distributed. The time limit for each pair of problems is six minutes. The first pair of problems is on the other side of this sheet. When told to do so, turn the page over and begin working. Record only final answers in the designated blanks on the problem sheet. All answers must be complete, legible, and simplified to lowest terms. This round assumes the use of calculators, and calculations may also be done on scratch paper, but no other aids are allowed. If you complete the problems before time is called, use the time remaining to check your answers.

Total Correct	Scorer's Initials

Copyright MYMATHCOUNTS.COM. All rights reserved.

Twenty Mathcounts Target Round Tests **Test 1**

1. _____ Given triangle *ABC* as shown, one of the 5 segments, *AB, BC, CD, DA,* and *BD* is selected at random. A second segment is selected from the remaining four. What is the probability, expressed as a fraction, that the segments picked, in order, have lengths in the ratio 4:3 or 3:2?

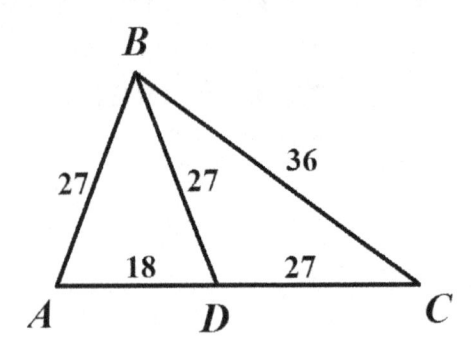

```
              B
             /|\
         27 / |27\ 36
           /  |    \
          /18 | 27   \
         A    D        C
```

2. _____ An equilateral triangle can be formed by four smaller equilateral triangles. Find the perimeter of the equilateral triangle if the area of each smaller triangle is $25\sqrt{3}$.

3. _____ A telephone line 100 feet long is related to a coordinate system as shown in the figure. A bird lands at $C(9)$, a second bird lands at $D(81)$, and a third bird lands at $E(45)$. After this, birds must observe the "right of free space" of birds already on the line. An approaching bird must land at the midpoint of the longest segment available. If two segments are of equal length, the bird must select the one to the right. What is the sum of the coordinates of the points where the fifth and sixth birds must land? Express your answer as a decimal to the nearest tenth.

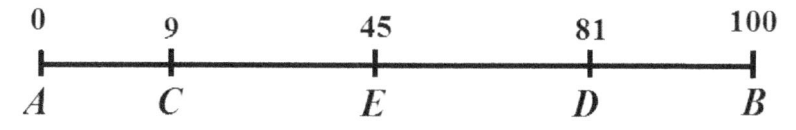

```
0        9           45          81         100
|--------|-----------|-----------|----------|
A        C           E           D          B
```

4. _____ A bag contains 5 blue marbles, 4 white marbles, and 3 red marbles. If three marbles are randomly selected from the bag, what is the probability that two of the three marbles selected will have the same color?

5. _____ Find the smallest positive integer that has 2 as a remainder when divided by 3, 4, 5, 6, 7, 8, 9.

6. _____ Any number of congruent, regular polygons (like the squares below) can be chained as shown.

Two hundred and one congruent, regular heptagons are chained in a similar manner. The resulting figure has a perimeter of 2014 centimeters. What is x, the length, in centimeters, of a side of one of the heptagons?

7. _____ A rectangle with the length p is inscribed in a circle of radius 8 inches. Find the area inside the circle but outside the rectangle, in square inches, expressed as a function of p.

8. _____ The eight integers, 1 through 8, are placed in the eight squares below, one integer per square, so that no two consecutive numbers are touching horizontally, vertically or diagonally. What number is placed in square B?

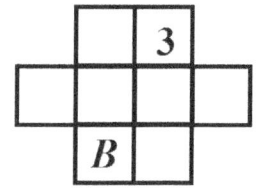

Twenty Mathcounts Target Round Tests — Test 1

SOLUTIONS:

Problem 1: 3/10.
$36 = 2^2 \times 3^2$; $27 = 3^3$; $18 = 2 \times 3^2$.
If the ratio is 4:3, we need to have 36. This line segment goes with three segments of 27. So we have 3 ways.
If the ratio is 3:2, we need to have 27. Three line segments with the length of 27 go with the line segment 18. So we have 3 more ways.
Total number of ways is $3 + 3 = 6$.
We have 5 ways to select the first line segment and 4 ways to select the second line segment.
The probability is $6/20 = 3/10$.

Problem 2: Solution: 60.
The area of an equilateral triangle is given by $\frac{1}{4}a^2\sqrt{3}$, where a is the side length of the triangle.
$\frac{1}{4}a^2\sqrt{3} = 25\sqrt{3} \implies a^2 = 100 \implies a = 10$.
The length of the sides of the larger triangle is $2 \times 10 = 20$.
The perimeter of the larger triangle is $3 \times 20 = 60$.

Problem 3: Solution: 117.5.
We place 3 birds on the line (b_1, b_2, and b_3) and calculate the distances for each segment:

The fourth bird will land 18 feet on the right of E.

The fifth bird will land 18 feet on the right of C. The coordinate is $9 + 18 = 27$.

Twenty Mathcounts Target Round Tests — Test 1

![number line diagram with points A, C, E, D, B and birds b_1, b_5, b_3, b_4, b_2 at positions 9, 45, 81, 100]

The sixth bird will land 19/2 feet on the right of D.

![number line diagram with points A, C, E, D, B and birds b_1, b_5, b_3, b_4, b_2, b_6]

The coordinate of the point where the sixth bird must land is $81 + 19/2 = 90.5$
The answer is $27 + 90.5 = 117.5$.

Problem 4: Solution: $\dfrac{29}{44}$.

We have three cases:

Case 1: Two blue marbles and one marble of other color:

$$P_1 = \frac{\binom{5}{2} \times \binom{7}{1}}{\binom{12}{3}} = \frac{7}{22}.$$

Case 2: Two red marbles and one marble of other color:

$$P_2 = \frac{\binom{4}{2} \times \binom{8}{1}}{\binom{12}{3}} = \frac{12}{55}.$$

Case 3: Two white marbles and one marble of other color:

$$P_3 = \frac{\binom{3}{2} \times \binom{9}{1}}{\binom{12}{3}} = \frac{27}{220}.$$

The answer is $P = P_1 + P_2 + P_3 = \dfrac{7}{22} + \dfrac{12}{55} + \dfrac{27}{220} = \dfrac{29}{44}$.

Twenty Mathcounts Target Round Tests — Test 1

Problem 5: Solution: 2522.

The number will have a remainder 2 when divided by the lcm (3, 4, 5, 6, 7, 8, 9) = 2520. So the number is 2520 + 2 = 2522.

Problem 6. Solution: 2.

A heptagon is a polygon with seven sides and seven angles.

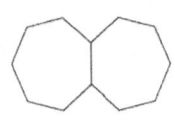

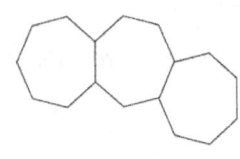

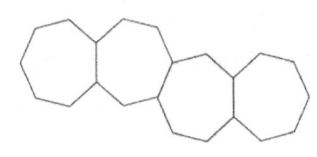

| 7 | 7 + 7 − 2 | 7 + 7 + 7 − 2 − 2 | 7 + 7 + 7 + 7 − 2 − 2 − 2 |

The perimeter is $P = [7n − 2(n − 1)] x = (5n + 2) x$, where n is the number of heptagon.

$(5 \times 201 + 2) x = 2014 \quad \Rightarrow \quad x = 2.$

Problem 7: Solution: $64\pi - p\sqrt{16^2 - p^2}$.

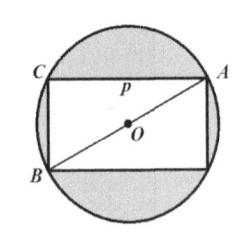

Applying Pythagorean Theorem to right triangle ABC:

$AC^2 + BC^2 = AB^2 \quad \Rightarrow \quad p^2 + BC^2 = 16^2 \quad \Rightarrow \quad BC = \sqrt{16^2 - p^2}$.

The shaded area = the area of the circle - the area of the rectangle

$= \pi \times r^2 - AC \times BC = \pi \times r^2 - p\sqrt{16^2 - p^2} = 64\pi - p\sqrt{16^2 - p^2}$.

Problem 8: Solution: 6.

First thing we need to realize is that only digits 1 and 8 can go to the two middle squares. We have only two cases:

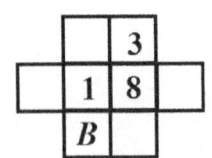

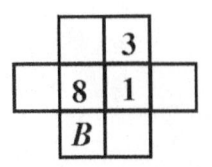

	3					3	
1	8				8	1	
	B					B	

For case 1, the number 2 has no square to go. This one does not work.

Twenty Mathcounts Target Round Tests — Test 1

For case 2, 2 can only go the left most square:

		3	
2	8	1	
	B		

We have digits 4, 5, 6, and 7 left. 7 can only go to the left most square:

		3	
2	8	1	7
	B		

4 can be placed in B or the square next to B.

Sub case 1: If B is 4 as shown, we have digits 5 and 6 left. We have no way to fit them in. This sub case does not work.

		3	
2	8	1	7
	4		

Sub case 2: We place 4 as shown in the figure. We have digits 5, and 6 left.

		3	
2	8	1	7
	B	4	

They fit in:

	5	3	
2	8	1	7
	6	4	

The answer is then $B = 6$.

Twenty Mathcounts Target Round Tests   **Test 2**

MATHCOUNTS

■ Mock Competition Two ■

Target Round

Name _____

State _____

DO NOT BEGIN UNTIL YOU ARE INSTRUCTED TO DO SO.

This section of the competition consists of eight problems, which will be presented in pairs. Work on one pair of problems will be completed and answers will be collected before the next pair is distributed. The time limit for each pair of problems is six minutes. The first pair of problems is on the other side of this sheet. When told to do so, turn the page over and begin working. Record only final answers in the designated blanks on the problem sheet. All answers must be complete, legible, and simplified to lowest terms. This round assumes the use of calculators, and calculations may also be done on scratch paper, but no other aids are allowed. If you complete the problems before time is called, use the time remaining to check your answers.

Total Correct	Scorer's Initials

Copyright   MYMATHCOUNTS.COM. All rights reserved.

Twenty Mathcounts Target Round Tests   **Test 2**

1. _____ Remove one integer from the list of n consecutive positive integers 1, 2, 3, ... n. The sum of the rest $(n-1)$ integers is 2014. Find the integer that is removed from the list.

2. _____ The base of the net is a square with the side length of 4. Four triangles are equilateral triangles. If this net is folded into a pyramid solid figure, what will be the height of the pyramid?

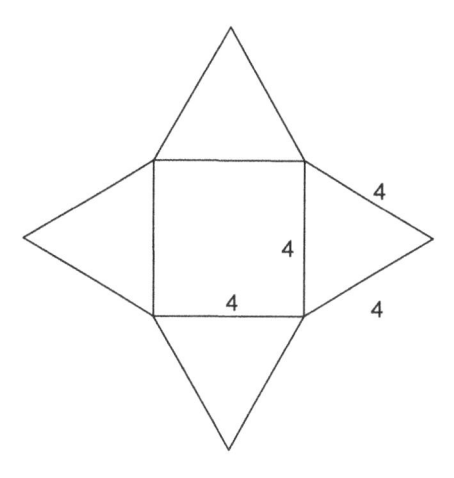

3. _____ List the numbers 1, 2, 3,…, 18 as shown. If we take one number from each row, and add these three numbers together, we get a number that is a multiple of 6. How many ways are there to do so?

1   2   3   4   5   6
7   8   9   10   11   12
13   14   15   16   17   18

4. _____ The diameter of the circle O is 10. $ABCD$ is a rectangle inscribed in O. $3\overline{AB} = 2\overline{AD}$. If we use the length of each side of $ABCD$ as the diameter to draw half circles as shown, what is the sum of the all shaded regions?

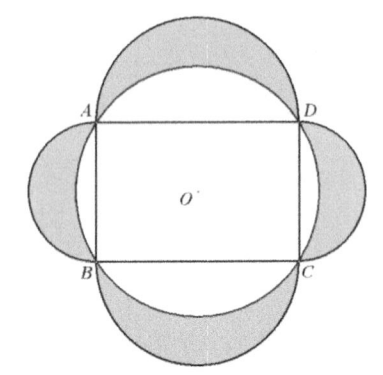

Twenty Mathcounts Target Round Tests Test 2

5. _____ Among the one hundred numbers 1^2, 2^2, $3^2, \cdots, 99^2$, 100^2, how many of them have an odd number as the tens digit?

6. _____ When 732 is divided by a natural number x, the remainder is 12. How many values of x are there?

Twenty Mathcounts Target Round Tests   Test 2

7. _____ Given $f(x) = \dfrac{101}{x+1}$, then what is the value of

$f(1) + f(2) + f(3) + f(4) + f(5) + f(\dfrac{1}{1}) + f(\dfrac{1}{2}) + f(\dfrac{1}{3}) + f(\dfrac{1}{4}) + f(\dfrac{1}{5})$?

8. _____ A division is shown as follows. Each square represents a digit. Find the quotient.

Twenty Mathcounts Target Round Tests   **Test 2**

SOLUTIONS:

Problem 1: Solution: 2.

Let the number be x. W have

$$1 + 2 + \cdots + (n-1) \leq (1 + 2 + 3 + \cdots + n) - x \leq 2 + 3 + \cdots + n$$

$$\Rightarrow \frac{n(n-1)}{2} \leq 2014 \leq \frac{(n+2)(n-1)}{2} \quad \Rightarrow n(n-1) \leq 4028 \leq (n+2)(n-1)..$$

We know that $\sqrt{4028} = 63.4\cdots$.

We try $n = 64 \Rightarrow n(n-1) = 64 \times 63 = 4032 > 4028$ that is too big.

We try $n = 63 \Rightarrow n(n-1) = 63 \times 62 = 3906 < 4028$ and

$(n+2)(n-1) = 65 \times 62 = 4030 > 4028$.

So we know that $n = 63$.

$x = 1 + 2 + \cdots + 63 - 2014 = \frac{63 \times 64}{2} - 2014 = 2$.

Problem 2: Solution:

We fold the pyramid as shown in the figure.

$\overline{AE} = \overline{EB} = 2$, $\overline{PE} = \sqrt{4^2 - 2^2} = \sqrt{12}$, $\overline{EO} = 2$

$\Rightarrow \overline{PO} = \sqrt{\sqrt{12}^2 - 2^2} = 2\sqrt{2}$

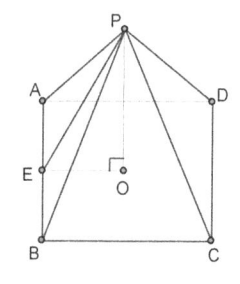

Problem 3: Solution: 36.

Let (a, b, c) be the remainder when the three numbers divided by 6. The following case will work:

(0, 0, 0)	1 way
(0, 1, 5)	6 ways
(0, 2, 4)	6 ways
(0, 3, 3)	3 ways
(1, 1, 4)	3 ways
(1, 2, 3)	6 ways
(2, 2, 2)	1 way

Twenty Mathcounts Target Round Tests — Test 2

(2, 5, 5)   3 ways
(3, 4, 5)   6 ways
(4, 4, 4)   1 way
Total $6 \times 4 + 3 \times 3 + 1 \times 3 = 36$ ways.

Problem 4: Solution:
Method 1:
Since $\overline{AB} : \overline{AD} = 2 : 3$, let $\overline{AB} = 2t$, $\overline{AD} = 3t$.

Applying Pythagorean Theorem to right triangle ABD, we have $t^2 + (\frac{3t}{2})^2 = 5^2 \Rightarrow$

$t^2 = \frac{100}{13}$.

The shaded area = the area of the circle with the diameter AD + the area of the circle with the diameter AB + the area of $ABCD$ − the area of the circle with the diameter AC

$= \pi t^2 + \pi(\frac{3}{2}t)^2 + 3t \cdot 2t - \pi \times 5^2 = \pi[t^2 + (\frac{3t}{2})^2 - 5^2] + 6t^2 = 6t^2 = \frac{600}{13}$.

Method 2:
We know that if A_1, A_2 and A_3 represent the areas of corresponding shaded regions, then $A_1 + A_2 = A_3$.

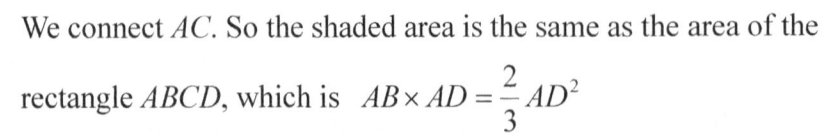

We connect AC. So the shaded area is the same as the area of the rectangle $ABCD$, which is $AB \times AD = \frac{2}{3} AD^2$

By Pythagorean Theorem, we have $AB^2 + AD^2 = 10^2$.
We also know that $AB = \frac{2}{3} AD$.

Thus $(\frac{2}{3} AD)^2 + AD^2 = 100 \Rightarrow \frac{13}{9} AD^2 = 100$.

Therefore $\frac{2}{3} AD^2 = \frac{600}{13}$.

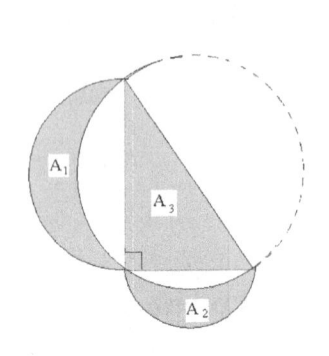

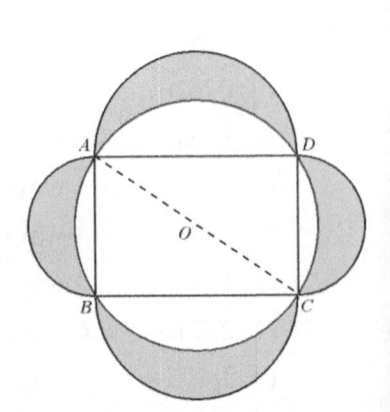

Twenty Mathcounts Target Round Tests — Test 2

Problem 5: Solution: 20.

We see that $(10n + a)^2 = 100n^2 + 20na + a^2$.

Since $20na$ is an even number, the parity of the tens digit of $(10n + a)^2$ is determined by the parity of the tens digit of a^2.

We also know that $1^2 = 1$, $2^2 = 4$, $3^2 = 9$, $4^2 = 16$, $5^2 = 25$, $6^2 = 36$, $7^2 = 49$, $8^2 = 64$, $9^2 = 81$, $10^2 = 100$.

There are two numbers that the tens digit is odd: 4^2, 6^2. Since we have 100 numbers that can be divided into 10 such groups, the answer is $2 \times 10 = 20$.

Problem 6: Solution: 20.

Because the remainder when 732 is divided by x is 12, we know that x is at least 13. Wecan subtract 12 from 732 to find a number that leaves a remainder of 0 when divided by 12. $732 - 12 = 720$ and $720 = 2^4 \times 3^2 \times 5$.

There are $(4 + 1) \times (2 + 1) \times (1 + 1) = 30$ factors of 720. Among them, we must subtract the factors that are less than 13, because they will leave a remainder less than 12. There are 10 factors of them: 1, 2, 3, 4, 5, 6, 8, 9, 10, and 12. The answer is $30 - 10 = 20$.

Problem 7: Solution: 505.

$$f(x) + f(\frac{1}{x}) = \frac{101}{x+1} + \frac{101}{\frac{1}{x}+1} = \frac{101}{x+1} + \frac{101x}{1+x} = \frac{101 + 101x}{x+1} = 101.$$

So the answer is $101 \times 5 = 505$.

Problem 8: Solution: 163.

We label each square as follows:

We see that $D \times A$ at most is 1. So $A = 1$ and $D = 1$.

G must be 2.

We know that $537 = 3 \times 179$. So the divisor is 179.

And F is 3.

We know that only 9×6 gives the units digit 4. So E is 6.

The quotient is then 163.

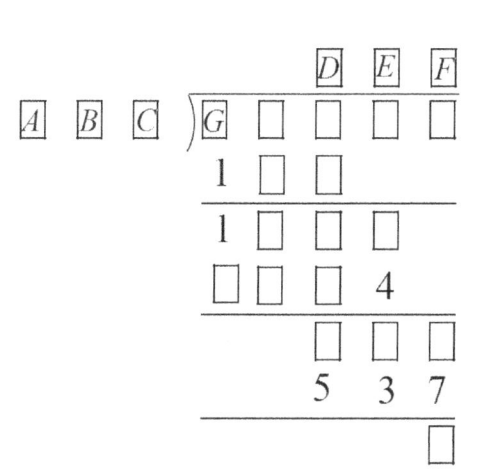

Twenty Mathcounts Target Round Tests   Test 3

MATHCOUNTS

■ Mock Competition Three ■

Target Round

Name _____

State _____

DO NOT BEGIN UNTIL YOU ARE INSTRUCTED TO DO SO.

This section of the competition consists of eight problems, which will be presented in pairs. Work on one pair of problems will be completed and answers will be collected before the next pair is distributed. The time limit for each pair of problems is six minutes. The first pair of problems is on the other side of this sheet. When told to do so, turn the page over and begin working. Record only final answers in the designated blanks on the problem sheet. All answers must be complete, legible, and simplified to lowest terms. This round assumes the use of calculators, and calculations may also be done on scratch paper, but no other aids are allowed. If you complete the problems before time is called, use the time remaining to check your answers.

Total Correct	Scorer's Initials

Copyright   MYMATHCOUNTS.COM. All rights reserved.

Twenty Mathcounts Target Round Tests — Test 3

1. _____ A square, 8 cm on each side, has four quarter circles drawn with centers at the four corners. How many square centimeters are in the area of the shaded region? Express your answer in the decimal form to the nearest tenth.

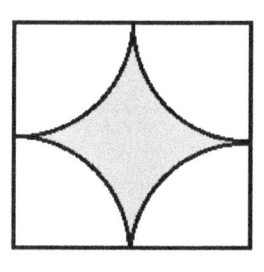

2. _____ A herbicide loses one-half of its toxic effect each week. After how many weeks will the herbicide have less than 1% of its original potency?

Twenty Mathcounts Target Round Tests   **Test 3**

3. _____ If the number of peanuts in a carton is divided by 15, 16, 17, 18, 19, and 20, there is two left over each time. What is the smallest number of peanuts, greater than one, that could be in the carton?

4. _____ If x and y are two different digits and z is any natural number, for how many combinations of x and y will $(10^z)x + y$ be divisible by 18?

Twenty Mathcounts Target Round Tests Test 3

5. _____ A five-digit number that is divisible by 6 is to be formed with five distinct digits. What is the largest possible number that can be formed if three of its digits are 5, 7, and 9?

6. _____ Given $f(x) = -|x-5|$ and $g(x) = \frac{1}{2}x^2 - 17$, for how many integral values of x is $g(x) < f(x)$?

7. _____ A 7 × 7 × 7 cube is formed by arranging 1 × 1 × 1 cubes. The faces of the large cube are then painted green. How many 1 × 1 × 1 cubes have at least two green faces?

8. _____ Three standard dice are rolled and their face values multiplied. What is the probability that the product is prime or ends in 6? Express your answer as a common fraction.

Twenty Mathcounts Target Round Tests — Test 3

SOLUTIONS:

Problem 1: 13.7

The shaded area is the same as the difference of the areas of the square and one circle as shown in the figure.

$8^2 - \dfrac{1}{4}\pi \times 8^2 = 64 - 16\pi \approx 13.7$.

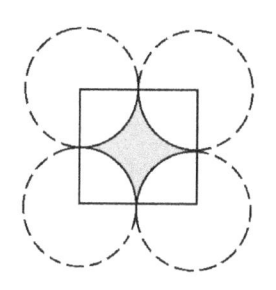

Problem 2: Solution: 7.

Let the original potency be x, and n be the number of weeks when the herbicide has less than 1% of its original potency.

$x(\dfrac{1}{2})^n < \dfrac{1}{100} \times x \quad \Rightarrow \quad (\dfrac{1}{2})^n < \dfrac{1}{100}$

When $n = 7$, $(\dfrac{1}{2})^7 = \dfrac{1}{128} < \dfrac{1}{100}$.

Problem 3: Solution: 232562.

We need to find the least common multiple of 15, 16, 17, 18, 19, and 20.

$15 = 3 \times 5$
$16 = 2^4$
$17 = 17$
$18 = 2 \times 3^2$
$19 = 19$
$20 = 2^2 \times 5$

lcm (15, 16, 17, 18, 19, 20) = $3^2 \times 2^4 \times 5 \times 17 \times 19$ = 232560.
The answer is then 232560 + 2 = 232562.

Problem 4: Solution:

Since the number is divisible by 18, it is divisible by 2 and 9. Thus the last digit of the number must be even, and the sum of its digits must be divisible by 9.
We have two cases:
Case 1: $x + y = 9$ and y is even.

We have the following 5 combinations of x and y will $(10^2)x + y$ be divisible by 18.
$x = 9, y = 0$.
$x = 7, y = 2$.
$x = 5, y = 4$.
$x = 3, y = 6$.
$x = 1, y = 8$.

Case 2: $x + y = 18$ and y is even.
We have no combinations for this case.
The answer is then 5.

Problem 5: Solution: 98754.
If a number is divisible by 6, the sum of its digits must be divisible by 3 and the last digit must be even. Let the fourth digit be a and the last digit be b.
$9 + 7 + 5 + a + b = 21 + a + b$.
So $a + b$ must be divisible by 3 and b must be even.
Since we want the largest possible number, we let $a = 8$ and $b = 4$.
So the number is 98754 (not 97584).

Problem 6. Solution: 9.

Since $g(x) < f(x)$, we have $\frac{1}{2}x^2 - 17 < -|x - 5|$.

So $\frac{1}{2}x^2 - 17 + |x - 5| < 0$.

When $x = 5$, we see that the inequality is true.
We have two more cases:

Case 1: $x > 5$.
$\frac{1}{2}x^2 - 17 + |x - 5| < 0 \implies \frac{1}{2}x^2 - 17 + x - 5 < 0 \implies \frac{1}{2}x^2 + x - 12 < 0$
$\implies x^2 + 2x - 24 < 0 \implies (x - 4)(x + 6) < 0$.
Since $x > 5$, we see no solutions for this inequality.

Case 2: $x < 5$.

$\frac{1}{2}x^2 - 17 + |x-5| < 0 \Rightarrow \frac{1}{2}x^2 - 17 + 5 - x < 0 \Rightarrow \frac{1}{2}x^2 - x - 12 < 0$

$\Rightarrow x^2 - 2x - 24 < 0 \Rightarrow (x-6)(x+4) < 0 \Rightarrow -4 < x < 6$.

The solutions are −3, −2, −1, 0, 1, 2, 3, 4, and 5 as shown in the figure.

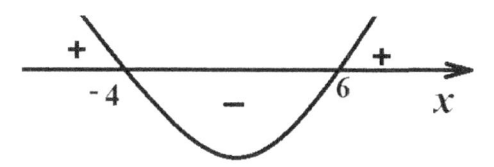

Considering the condition $x < 5$, we get 8 solutions (−3, −2, −1, 0, 1, 2, 3, 4).
Total we have 1 + 8 = 9 solutions.

Problem 7: Solution: 68.

Method 1:

From the table, that the number of cubes with at least two faces painted is 8 + 60 = 68

Cube dimension	7 × 7 × 7	$n \times n \times n$
3 sides painted	8	8
2 sides painted	60	$(n-2)^1 \times 2 \times 6$
1 sides painted	150	$(n-2)^2 \times 1 \times 6$
0 sides painted	125	$(n-2)^3$
Total number of cubes	343	n^3

Method 2:

There are 5 × 5 × 6 = 150 cubes painted one face only.

When we peel off six exterior layers of the large cube, we get the number of cubes painted no faces: $(7-2) \times (7-2) \times (7-2) = 5^3$ = 125.

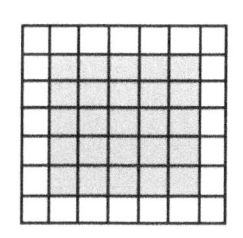

The number of cubes with at least two faces painted is 7^3 − 150 − 125 = 68.

Problem 8: Solution: $\frac{5}{27}$.

We have two cases.

Case 1: the product is a prime.

1	1	2	(3 combinations)
1	1	3	(3 combinations)
1	1	5	(3 combinations)

Case 2: the product ends in 6.

1	1	6	(3 combinations)
1	2	3	(6 combinations)
1	4	4	(3 combinations)
1	6	6	(3 combinations)
2	3	6	(6 combinations)
4	4	6	(3 combinations)
6	6	6	(1 combination)
2	2	4	(3 combinations)
3	3	4	(3 combinations)

$3 \times 9 + 6 \times 2 + 1 = 40$.

The probability is $P = \frac{40}{6^3} = \frac{5}{27}$.

MATHCOUNTS

■ Mock Competition Four ■

Target Round

Name _____

State _____

DO NOT BEGIN UNTIL YOU ARE INSTRUCTED TO DO SO.

This section of the competition consists of eight problems, which will be presented in pairs. Work on one pair of problems will be completed and answers will be collected before the next pair is distributed. The time limit for each pair of problems is six minutes. The first pair of problems is on the other side of this sheet. When told to do so, turn the page over and begin working. Record only final answers in the designated blanks on the problem sheet. All answers must be complete, legible, and simplified to lowest terms. This round assumes the use of calculators, and calculations may also be done on scratch paper, but no other aids are allowed. If you complete the problems before time is called, use the time remaining to check your answers.

Total Correct	Scorer's Initials

Copyright   MYMATHCOUNTS.COM. All rights reserved.

Twenty Mathcounts Target Round Tests — Test 4

1. _____ Three positive numbers a, b, and c from an arithmetic sequence and $a + b + c = 27$. If $a + 2$, $b + 3$, and $c + 10$ form a geometric sequence, find the smallest value among a, b, and c.

2. _____ As shown in the figure, M is the midpoint of AD, $MN \perp AD$. Find the length of CN if $AB//CD$, $\angle ABC = 90°$. $AB = 13$, $BC = 12$, and $CD = 11$.

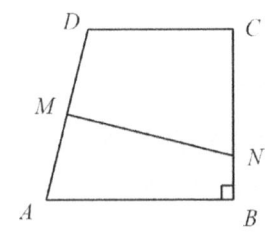

3. _____ As shown in the figure, *ABCD* is a rectangle. *AB* =16, *AD* = 18. Two circles have the same diameters and are tangent to the sides of the rectangle. Find the radius of the circle O_1.

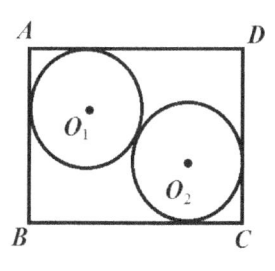

4. _____ You have 24 bills of $10, $20, and $50 with each denomination at least one bill. The amount of them is $1,000. How many are $20 bills?

Twenty Mathcounts Target Round Tests   **Test 4**

5. _____ As shown in the figure, $\triangle ABC$ is an equilateral triangle. $BN = \frac{1}{4}AB$, $BM = \frac{1}{4}BC$, $AF = FE = ED = DC = \frac{1}{4}AB$. Find $\angle 1 + \angle 2 + \angle 3$.

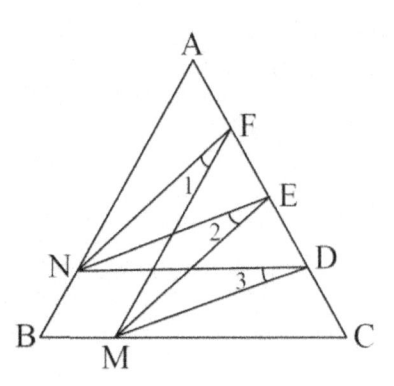

6. _____ A two-digit positive integer satisfies the following conditions:
(1) The difference between 2 times the units digit and the tens digit is larger than 2, and
(2) The sum of 3 times the tens digit and the units digit is less than 25.
What is the greatest possible value of such two-digit number?

7. _____ A closet contains 4 pairs of shoes (therefore a total of 8 shoes). Assume that 4 shoes are chosen at random without replacement. What is the probability that there will be no matching pairs? Express your answer as a simplest fraction).

8. _____ Alex, Bob, Charles, Danny, and Emma weigh each a, b, c, d, and e pounds, respectively. Find the heaviest person if the following inequalities hold. $a+b<c+d, b+c<d+e, c+d<e+a,$ and $d+e<a+b$.

Twenty Mathcounts Target Round Tests   Test 4

SOLUTIONS:

Problem 1: Solution: 4.

b is $27/3 = 9$.

Let three numbers be $9-d, 9, 9+d \Rightarrow 11-d, 12, 19+d$ form a geometric sequence.

$12^2 = (11-d)(19+d) \Rightarrow d^2 + 8d - 65 = 0$

Solve we get $d = 5$ or -13 (ignored).

Thus three numbers are 4, 9, 14. The smallest one is 4.

Problem 2: Solution: 8.

Connect $\overline{DN}$ and $\overline{AN}$.

Since $DM = MA$, and MN is the height of triangle AND, $\overline{DN} = \overline{AN}$.

Let $\overline{CN} = x \Rightarrow \overline{BN} = 12 - x$.

$11^2 + x^2 = (12-x)^2 + 13^2 \Rightarrow x = 8, \overline{CN} = 8$.

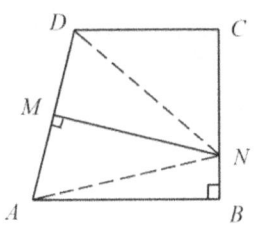

Problem 3: Solution: 5.

$\overline{O_1O_2} = 2r, \overline{EO_1} = 18 - 2r, \overline{EO_2} = 16 - 2r$.

Applying Pythagorean Theorem to ΔO_1EO_2:

$\Rightarrow (18-2r)^2 + (16-2r)^2 = (2r)^2 \Rightarrow$

$r^2 - 34r + 145 = 0$.

Solving we get: $r = 5$ or 29 (ignored)

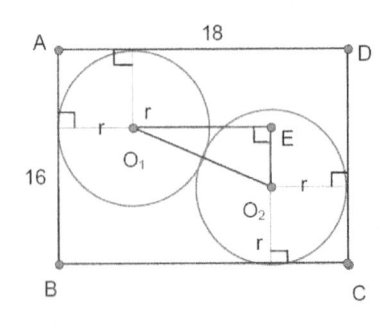

Problem 4: Solution: 4.

Let x, y, and z be the number of bills of $10, $20, and $50 respectively.

$10x + 20y + 50z = 1000$ (1)

Or $x + 2y + 5z = 100$ (2)

$x + y + z = 24$ (3)

(2) – (3): $y + 4z = 76$ (4)

If $y = 4$, $z = 18$, and $x = 2$. The solution works.

It is easy to check that all other values of y (8, 12, 16, ,..) will not work.

Problem 5: Solution: 60.

Connect $\overline{NM}$.

Since $\overline{BN} = \frac{1}{4}\overline{AB}, \overline{BM} = \frac{1}{4}\overline{BC}$, $\overline{NM} \, // \, \overline{AC}$ and $\overline{NM} = \frac{1}{4}\overline{AC}$.

We also know that $\overline{AF} = \overline{FE} = \overline{ED}$. So $NMFA, NMEF, NMDE$ are all parallelograms. Thus $\angle 1 = \angle ANF, \angle 2 = \angle FNE, \angle 3 = \angle END$.

Therefore $\angle 1 + \angle 2 + \angle 3 = \angle AND = \angle ABC = 60°$.

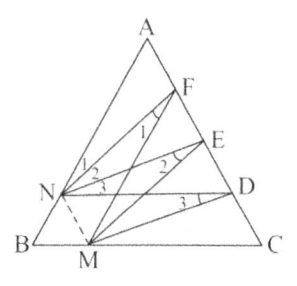

Problem 6: Solution: 66.

Let x, y be the tens and the units digits of the number, respectively.

We have

$2y - x > 2$ (1)

$3x + y < 25$ (2)

We write (2) as $50 > 6x + 2y$ (3)

$(1) + (3)$: $2y - x + 50 > 2 + 6x + 2y \Rightarrow \quad 7x < 48 \quad \Rightarrow \quad x < \frac{48}{7} \leq 6$.

Since we want the greatest value, we let $x = 6$.

If $x = 6$,

$2y - 6 > 2 \quad \Rightarrow \quad 2y > 8 \quad \Rightarrow \quad y > 4$

$3x + y < 25 \quad \Rightarrow \quad y < 7$

y can be 5, or 6.

The number can be 65 or 66. Since we want the greatest one, 66 is our answer.

Problem 7: Solution: 8/35.

Let the 4 pairs of shoes be:

$A_1 \quad B_1 \quad C_1 \quad D_1$

$A_2 \quad B_2 \quad C_2 \quad D_2$

The cases that no matching pairs:

Case 1: Select 4 shoes from the first row or from the second row:

Twenty Mathcounts Target Round Tests   **Test 4**

$$\boxed{A_1\ B_1\ C_1\ D_1} \\ \boxed{A_2\ B_2\ C_2\ D_2}$$ or $$\boxed{A_1\ B_1\ C_1\ D_1 \\ A_2\ B_2\ C_2\ D_2}$$

The number of ways: $2 \times \binom{4}{1}$.

Case 2: Select 3 shoes from the first row and 1 from the second row or select 3 shoes from the second row and 1 from the first row:

$$\boxed{A_1\ B_1\ C_1}D_1 \\ A_2\ B_2\ C_2\boxed{D_2}$$

The number of ways: $2 \times \binom{4}{3}$.

Case 3: Select 4 shoes from the first row and 2 from 4 of the second row.

$$A_1\ \boxed{B_1}\ C_1\ D_1 \\ A_2\ B_2\ \boxed{C_2\ D_2}$$

The number of ways: $\binom{4}{2}$.

The number of ways no matching pairs: $2\binom{4}{4} + 2\binom{4}{3} + \binom{4}{2} = 16$

The total ways: $\binom{8}{4} = 70$.

The probability is $\dfrac{16}{70} = \dfrac{8}{35}$.

Method 2:

Let the 4 pairs of shoes be:

$A_1\ \ B_1\ \ C_1\ \ D_1$
$A_2\ \ B_2\ \ C_2\ \ D_2$

Step 1: We can pick up any one of these 8 shoes. So the chance is 1.
Step 2: Let us say we picked A_1 in step 1. We have 7 shoes left.

A_1 B_1 C_1 D_1
A_2 B_2 C_2 D_2

Now we can pick up any shoes from the rest of shoes except A_2. So the probability is $\frac{6}{7}$.

Step 3: Let us say we picked B_1 in step 2. We have 6 shoes left.

$\cancel{A_1}$ $\cancel{B_1}$ C_1 D_1
A_2 B_2 C_2 D_2

Now we can pick up any shoes from the rest of shoes except A_2 and B_2. So the probability is $\frac{4}{6}$.

Step 4: Let us say we picked C_1 in step 3. $\cancel{A_1}$ $\cancel{B_1}$ $\cancel{C_1}$ D_1
A_2 B_2 C_2 D_2

We have 5 shoes left. Now we can pick up D_1 or D_2. So the probability is $\frac{2}{5}$.

The answer is $1 \times \frac{6}{7} \times \frac{4}{6} \times \frac{2}{5} = \frac{8}{35}$.

Problem 8: Solution: Alex.

$$\begin{cases} a+b < c+d \cdots (1) \\ b+c < d+e \cdots (2) \\ c+d < e+a \cdots (3) \\ d+e < a+b \cdots (4) \end{cases}$$

$(1)+(3) \Rightarrow a+b+c+d < c+d+e+a \Rightarrow b < e$
$(1)+(4) \Rightarrow a+b+d+e < c+d+a+b \Rightarrow e < c$
$(2)+(4) \Rightarrow b+c+d+e < d+e+a+b \Rightarrow c < a$

So $a > c > e > b$

$(3)+(4) \Rightarrow c+2d+e < e+2a+b \Rightarrow c+2d < 2a+b$

Since $c > b$, $2d < 2a \Rightarrow d < a$

So Alex is the heaviest person.

MATHCOUNTS

■ Mock Competition Five ■

Target Round

Name _____

State _____

DO NOT BEGIN UNTIL YOU ARE INSTRUCTED TO DO SO.

This section of the competition consists of eight problems, which will be presented in pairs. Work on one pair of problems will be completed and answers will be collected before the next pair is distributed. The time limit for each pair of problems is six minutes. The first pair of problems is on the other side of this sheet. When told to do so, turn the page over and begin working. Record only final answers in the designated blanks on the problem sheet. All answers must be complete, legible, and simplified to lowest terms. This round assumes the use of calculators, and calculations may also be done on scratch paper, but no other aids are allowed. If you complete the problems before time is called, use the time remaining to check your answers.

Total Correct	Scorer's Initials

Copyright MYMATHCOUNTS.COM. All rights reserved.

Twenty Mathcounts Target Round Tests — Test 5

1. _____ The three consecutive digits a, b, and c are used to form the three-digit numbers *abc* and *cba*. What is the greatest common divisor of all numbers of the form *abc* + *cba*?

2. _____ In how many different ways may 11 indistinguishable dimes be distributed among Susan, Frank and Harold if each must receive at least one dime?

Twenty Mathcounts Target Round Tests — Test 5

3. _____ When Lauren was born on January 1, 2002, her grandparents put $1000 in a savings account in her name. The account earned 8% annual interest compounded quarterly on March 1, June 1, September 1 and December 1. To the nearest dollar, how much money was in her account on her 10th birthday?

4. _____ Two bags of marbles are pictured below. Five marbles are randomly selected from Bag *A* and placed into Bag *B*. One marble is then randomly selected from Bag *B*. What is the probability that the marble selected from Bag *B* is white?

Bag *A*   Bag *B*

38

Twenty Mathcounts Target Round Tests   **Test 5**

5. _____ In the figure shown, the circle with center at O has a radius of 4 and the square has side of length 9. If a point is selected at random from within the region determined by the circle and the square, what is the probability that it will be within the shaded region? Express your answer as a decimal rounded to the nearest hundredth. Use 3.14 for π.

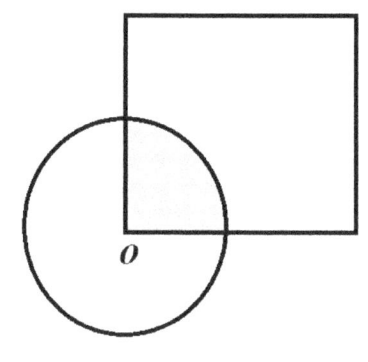

6. _____ If 112 is the remainder when a 4-digit positive integer is divided by 131, and 98 is the remainder when the 4-digit positive integer is divided by 132, find the 4-digit positive integer.

7. _____ When 2015 is divided by a 2-digit positive integer, what is the greatest possible remainder?

8. _____ $ABCD$ is an isosceles trapezoid with $AB//DC$. $BE \perp DC$ at E and $BE = AB$. Find AB if $DB = DC = 10$.

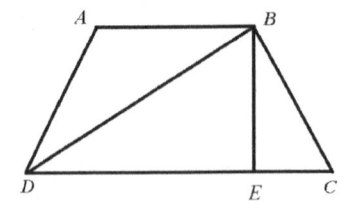

Twenty Mathcounts Target Round Tests — Test 5

SOLUTIONS:

Problem 1: Solution: 222.

Le $b = a + 1$, $c = a + 2$.

$abc + cba = 100a + 10b + c + 100c + 10b + a = 101a + 101c + 20b = 101(a + c) + 20b$
$= 101(a + a + 2) + 20(a + 1) = 202a + 202 + 20a + 20 = 222a + 222 = 222(a + 1)$.

So the greatest common divisor of all numbers of the form **abc + cba** is 222.

Problem 2: Solution: 45.

Method 1:

This question is the same as the following question:

How many ways are there to write 11 as three positive integers? $9 + 1 + 1$ and $1 + 1 + 9$ are considered two different ways.

So we write 11 as

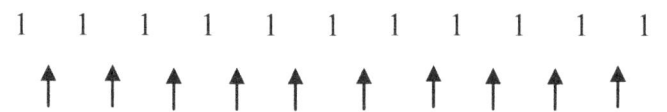

  1 1 1 1 1 1 1 1 1 1 1
  ↑ ↑ ↑ ↑ ↑ ↑ ↑ ↑ ↑ ↑

We have 10 partitions. Since we want to divide 11 as the sum of three positive integer, we only need 2 partition out of these two partitions.

We have the following ways to choose 2 partitions out of then: $\binom{10}{2} = \dfrac{10 \times 9}{2} = 45$.

Method 2:

This is integer solution problem. We set up the equation as

$s + f + h = 11$.

The number of positive integer solutions is $\binom{11-1}{3-1} = \binom{10}{2} = \dfrac{10 \times 9}{2} = 45$.

Problem 3: Solution: 2208.

We know that if P dollars are deposited in an account paying an annual rate of interest r compounded (paid) m times per year, then after t years the account will contain A dollars, where $A = P(1 + \dfrac{r}{m})^{tm}$.

Thus $A = 1000(1+\dfrac{0.08}{4})^{10\times 4} \approx 2208$.

Problem 4: Solution: 0.58.

Let B be the event that the marble selected from Bag B is white,

A_1 be the event selecting 4 black marbles and 1 white marble from Bag A,

B_1 be the event that the marble selected from Bag B is white after A_1,

A_2 be the event selecting 3 black marbles and 2 white marbles from Bag A,

B_2 be the event that the marble selected from Bag B is white after A_2,

A_3 be the event selecting 2 black marbles and 3 white marbles from Bag A,

B_3 be the event that the marble selected from Bag B is white after A_3.

$$B = A_1B_1 + A_2B_2 + A_3B_3$$

Then

$$P(B) = P(A_1B_1) + P(A_2B_2) + P(A_3B_3) = P(A_1)P(B_1|A_1) + P(A_2)P(B_2|A_2) + P(A_3)P(B_3|A_3)$$

$$P(A_1) = \dfrac{\binom{4}{4}\binom{3}{1}}{\binom{7}{5}}; \quad P(A_2) = \dfrac{\binom{4}{3}\binom{3}{2}}{\binom{7}{5}}; \quad P(A_3) = \dfrac{\binom{4}{2}\binom{3}{3}}{\binom{7}{5}}; \quad P(B_1|A_1) = \dfrac{6+1}{14}; \quad P(B_2|A_2) = \dfrac{6+2}{14};$$

$$P(B_3|A_3) = \dfrac{6+3}{14}.$$

$P(B) = 0.58$.

Problem 5: Solution: 0.11.

The probability is the ratio of the area of the shaded area/ the combined area =

$$\dfrac{\dfrac{\pi r^2}{4}}{9^2 + \pi r^2 - \dfrac{\pi r^2}{4}} = \dfrac{\dfrac{\pi \times 4^2}{4}}{9^2 + \pi \times 4^2 - \dfrac{\pi \times 4^2}{4}} \approx 0.11.$$

Problem 6. Solution: 1946.

Let the 4-digit positive integer be n.

$n = 132a + 98 = 131a + a + 98$.

(Note that when $n = 132a + 98 = 131a + a + 98$ is divided by 131, the remainder will be $a + 98$).

So $a + 98 = 131b + 112$ $\Rightarrow$ $a = 131b + 14$.

Therefore $n = 132(131b + 14) + 98 = 132 \times 131b + 1946$.

Since n is a 4-digit number, b must be zero and $n = 1946$.

Method 2:

$131a + 112 = 132b + 98$ $\Rightarrow$ $131a + 14 = 132b$ $\Rightarrow$ $14 \equiv b \pmod{131}$.

So $b = 14$ and $132b + 98 = 132 \times 14 + 98 = 1946$.

Problem 7: Solution: 95.

Since $2015 \div 99 = 20 \, R \, 35$, we are looking for R such that:

$2015 = 9? \times 20 + R$
$= 99 \times 20 + 35$
$= 98 \times 20 + 55$
$= 97 \times 20 + 75$
$= 96 \times 20 + 95$
$= 95 \times 20 + 115$

Note that 115 is a 3-digit divisor and is not counted.

The greatest possible remainder when 2015 is divided by a 2-digit positive integer is 95.

Problem 8: Solution: 6.

Method 1:

We know that in an isosceles trapezoid $ABCD$, the following relationship is true:

$BD^2 = AD^2 + AB \times CD$

So we have $10^2 = BC^2 + AB \times 10$ (1)

Draw $AF \perp DC$ at E. We know that

$BC^2 = BE^2 + EC^2 = AB^2 + \left(\dfrac{DC - AB}{2}\right)^2 = AB^2 + \left(\dfrac{10 - AB}{2}\right)^2$ (2)

Twenty Mathcounts Target Round Tests — Test 5

Substituting (2) into (1), we get:

$$10^2 = AB^2 + \left(\frac{10-AB}{2}\right)^2 + AB \times 10 \quad \Rightarrow$$

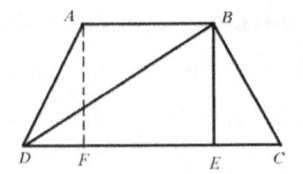

$$10^2 = AB^2 + \left(\frac{10-AB}{2}\right)^2 + AB \times 10$$

$\Rightarrow AB^2 + 4AB - 60 = 0$.

Solving the quadratic equation, we have $AB = 6$ or $AB = 10$ (extraneous, since $DB = DC = 10$).

Therefore $AB = 6$.

Method 2:

Connect AC and draw $BM//AC$ to meet DC at M.
Since $AB//DC$ and $BM//AC$, $AB = CM$, $AC = BM$.
Since $AD = BC$, $BD = AC$. Thus $BM = BD = 10$.
Since $BE \perp DC$, $DE = EM$.
We know that $DC = 10$. Let $DE = x$.
Then $CE = 10 - x$, $EM = x$.
So $CM = EM - CE = 2x - 10$.
We know that $BE = AB = CM$, so $BE = 2x - 10$.
By Pythagorean Theorem, we have $BE^2 + DE^2 = BD^2$, or $(2x-10)^2 + x^2 = 100$.
This can be simplified into $5x^2 - 40x = 0$.
Since $x > 0$, $x = 8$.
Therefore $AB = 2x - 10 = 6$.

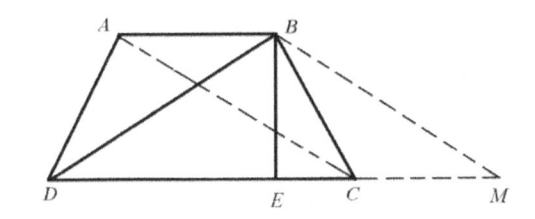

… Twenty Mathcounts Target Round Tests   Test 6

MATHCOUNTS

■ Mock Competition Six ■

Target Round

Name _____

State _____

DO NOT BEGIN UNTIL YOU ARE INSTRUCTED TO DO SO.

This section of the competition consists of eight problems, which will be presented in pairs. Work on one pair of problems will be completed and answers will be collected before the next pair is distributed. The time limit for each pair of problems is six minutes. The first pair of problems is on the other side of this sheet. When told to do so, turn the page over and begin working. Record only final answers in the designated blanks on the problem sheet. All answers must be complete, legible, and simplified to lowest terms. This round assumes the use of calculators, and calculations may also be done on scratch paper, but no other aids are allowed. If you complete the problems before time is called, use the time remaining to check your answers.

Total Correct	Scorer's Initials

Copyright   MYMATHCOUNTS.COM. All rights reserved.

Twenty Mathcounts Target Round Tests — Test 6

1. _____ Apple Store sells apples in two types of boxes: one contains 10 apples (cost: $20) and one contains 6 apples (cost: $10). Alex bought a number of boxes containing a total of 76 apples and paid a. Bob bought a different number of boxes but containing also 76 apples in total and paid b. What is the greatest positive difference between a and b?

2. _____ If a, b, c, and d are all positive integers $a^2 + b^2 = c^2 - d^2 = 281$ and with $a > b$, $c > d$. Find the value of $a + c$.

3. _____ There are four people in Alex's family (father, mother, younger sister and himself). The sum of the ages of four people is 93. Six times the father's age is 7 times the mother's age. The mother's age is three times Alex's age. If all ages are integers, find Alex's age.

4. _____ A box contains 11 balls, numbered 1, 2, 3, . . . , 11. If 6 balls are drawn simultaneously at random, what is the probability that the sum of the numbers drawn is odd? Express the answer as a common fraction.

Twenty Mathcounts Target Round Tests   **Test 6**

5. _____ Given that $\dfrac{x_1}{x_1+1} = \dfrac{x_2}{x_2+3} = \dfrac{x_3}{x_3+5} = \cdots\cdots = \dfrac{x_{10}}{x_{10}+19}$ and $x_1 + x_2 + x_3 + \ldots + x_{10} = 2015$. If $x_1 = \dfrac{n}{m}$, n and m are positive integers relatively prime, find the value of $m + n$.

6. _____ As shown in the figure, O is a point inside the square $ABCD$. Draw a circle by using O as the center, 12 as the radius. The circle meets AB at E, meets AD at F. The distance from O to AD is the same as that from O to AB and is $6\sqrt{3}$. The shaded area can be expressed as $c\pi$. Find the value of c.

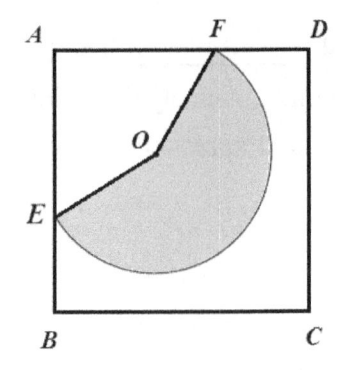

7. _____ For any positive integer k, $f(k)$ means the integer part of $\sqrt{k}$. For example, $f(3) = 1$, $f(5) = 2$, and $f(16) = 4$. If $f(1) + f(2) + f(3) + ... + f(n) = 231$, find the value of n.

8. _____ As shown in the figure, $\angle A = 90°$. $AB = 8$, $AC = 6$. $S_1, S_2, ..., S_7$ are all squares. Find the sum of perimeters of all seven squares.

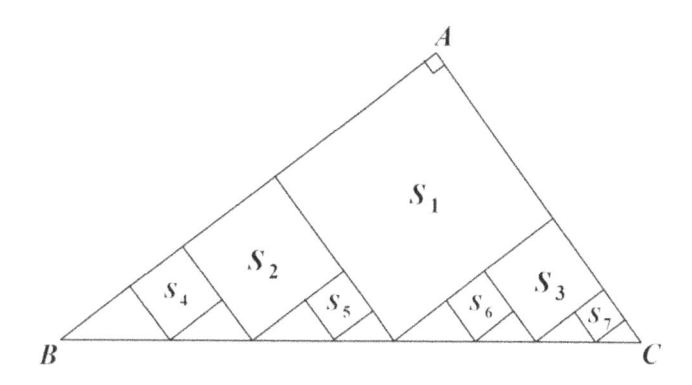

Twenty Mathcounts Target Round Tests — Test 6

SOLUTIONS:

Problem 1: Solution: 20.
Let x be the number of boxes containing 10 apples and y be the number of boxes containing 6 apples, M be the money paid.

$10x + 6y = 76 \quad \Rightarrow \quad 5x + 3y = 38$.
$M = 20x + 10y = 4(38 - 3y) + 10y = 152 - 2y$.

We assume that Alex paid the lowest possible price and Bob paid the highest possible price.

The lowest value of M occurs when y is the maximum, or $y = 11$.
$a = 152 - 22 = 130$.

The highest value of M occurs when y is the minimum, or $y = 1$.
$b = 152 - 2 = 150$.

The answer is $150 - 130 = 20$.

Problem 2: Solution: 157.
We know that $a^2 + b^2 = 281$ and $a > b$. $a^2 + a^2 > 281$ and $a > 11$.

We also know that $a^2 < 281$ and $a < \sqrt{281} \approx 16.76$. Since a is integer, $a \le 16$.

Let $a = 16$. $16^2 + b^2 = 281 \quad \Rightarrow \quad b^2 = 281 - 16^2 = 25 \quad \Rightarrow \quad b = 5$.

There are no integral values of b for $a = 12, 13, 14,$ or 15.
It is easy to check that 281 is a prime number. So $c^2 - d^2 = 281 \Rightarrow (c+d)(c-d) = 281 = 281 \times 1$.
We have:
$$\begin{cases} c + d = 281 \\ c - d = 1 \end{cases}$$
Solving we get $c = 141, d = 140$. Therefore $a + c = 16 + 141 = 157$.

Problem 3: Solution: 12.
Let the ages of Alex, sister, father, and mother be $a, s, f,$ and m, respectively.
We have:

Twenty Mathcounts Target Round Tests Test 6

$$a + s + f + m = 93 \qquad (1)$$
$$6f = 7m \qquad (2)$$
$$m = 3a \qquad (3)$$

We eliminate f and m in the system of equations:
$$15a + 2s = 186 \qquad (4)$$
We re-write (4) as
$$a = \frac{186 - 2s}{15} = \frac{180 + 6 - 2s}{15} = 12 + \frac{2(3-s)}{15}.$$

Since a and s are positive integers with $a > s$, $3 - s$ must be a multiple of 15. The only case is $s = 3$. (Note that s can also be 18, 33,.. but since $a > s$, we ignore these values). When $s = 3$, $a = 12$.

Problem 4: Solution: $\frac{118}{231}$.

We group the numbers as follows:

1 3 5 7 9 11
2 4 6 8 10

Case 1: We select 5 numbers from the first row and 1 number from the second row. The number of ways to do so is $\binom{6}{5}\binom{5}{1}$.

Case 2: We select 3 numbers from the first row and 3 number from the second row. The number of ways to do so is $\binom{6}{3}\binom{5}{3}$.

Case 2: We select 1 number from the first row and 5 number from the second row. The number of ways to do so is $\binom{6}{1}\binom{5}{5}$.

The total number of ways to select 5 numbers is $\binom{11}{6}$.

The probability is $\dfrac{\binom{6}{5}\binom{5}{1} + \binom{6}{3}\binom{5}{3} + \binom{6}{1}\binom{5}{5}}{\binom{11}{6}} = \dfrac{236}{462} = \dfrac{118}{231}.$

Twenty Mathcounts Target Round Tests — Test 6

Problem 5: Solution: 423.

Method 1:

$$\frac{x_1}{x_1+1} = \frac{x_2}{x_2+3} = \frac{x_3}{x_3+5} = \cdots = \frac{x_{10}}{x_{10}+19} = \frac{x_1+x_2+\ldots+x_{19}}{x_1+1+x_2+3+\ldots+x_{10}+19} = \frac{2015}{2015+10^2}$$

$$\frac{x_1}{x_1+1} = \frac{2015}{2015+10^2} \Rightarrow \frac{x_1+1}{x_1} = \frac{2015+10^2}{2015} \Rightarrow 1+\frac{1}{x_1} = 1+\frac{100}{2015} \Rightarrow x_1 = \frac{2015}{100} = \frac{403}{20}.$$

$m = 20, n = 403, m+n = 423$.

Method 2:

Let $\dfrac{x_1}{x_1+1} = \dfrac{x_2}{x_2+3} = \dfrac{x_3}{x_3+5} = \cdots = \dfrac{x_{10}}{x_{10}+19} = t$

Then $x_1 = \dfrac{t}{1-t}$, $x_2 = \dfrac{3t}{1-t}$, $x_3 = \dfrac{5t}{1-t}$, ..., $x_{10} = \dfrac{19t}{1-t}$.

$$\frac{t+3t+5t+\cdots+19t}{1-t} = 2015 \Rightarrow \frac{100t}{1-t} = 2015.$$

$x_1 = \dfrac{t}{1-t} = \dfrac{2015}{100} = \dfrac{403}{20}.$

$m = 20, n = 403, m+n = 423$.

Problem 6: Solution: 84.

Draw $\overline{OG} \perp \overline{AD}$ at G. $\overline{OH} \perp \overline{AB}$ at H. $\overline{OE} = \overline{OF} = 12$. $\overline{OG} = \overline{OH} = 6\sqrt{3}$.

Applying Pythagorean Theorem to $\triangle OHE$ and $\triangle OGF$, respectively:

$HE = \sqrt{OE^2 - OH^2} = \sqrt{12^2 - (6\sqrt{3})^2} = \sqrt{144-108} = \sqrt{36} = 6 = \dfrac{1}{2}OE$.

$GF = \sqrt{OF^2 - OG^2} = \sqrt{12^2 - (6\sqrt{3})^2} = \sqrt{144-108} = \sqrt{36} = 6 = \dfrac{1}{2}OF$.

Thus $\angle GOF = \angle HOE = 30°$.

We also know that $\angle HOG = 90°$.

So $\angle EOF = 360° - 90° - 30° - 30° = 210°$.

The shaded are is $\dfrac{360°}{\pi r^2} = \dfrac{210°}{x} \Rightarrow$

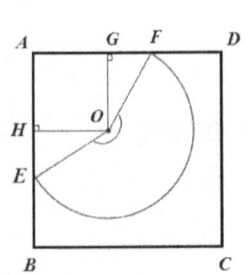

$$x = \frac{210°}{360°} \times \pi r^2 = \frac{210°}{360°} \times \pi \times 12^2 = \frac{7 \times 3}{3 \times 12} \times \pi \times 12 \times 12 = 84\pi$$

Therefore $c = 84$.

Problem 7: Solution: 52.

$f(1) + f(2) + f(3) = 1 \times 3$;

$f(4) + f(5) + f(6) + f(7) + f(8) = 2 \times 5$;

$f(9) + f(10) + f(11) + f(12) + (f(13) + f(14) + f(15) = 3 \times 7$.

We see that pattern so:

$1 \times 3 + 2 \times 5 + 3 \times 7 + 4 \times 9 + 5 \times 11 + 6 \times 13 + 7 \times 4 = 231$.

Thus $n = 3 + 5 + 7 + 9 + 11 + 13 + 4 = 52$.

Problem 8: Solution: $\frac{288}{7}$.

Let a_n be the side of S_n. We see that triangle BDE is similar to triangle BAC. So we have

$\frac{a_1}{6} = \frac{8-a_1}{8} = \frac{8}{14} = \frac{4}{7} \quad \Rightarrow \quad a_1 = \frac{24}{7}$.

Similarly, $\frac{a_2}{6} = \frac{8 - a_1 - a_2}{8} = \frac{8 - a_1}{14} \quad \Rightarrow \quad 7a_2 = 24 - 3a_1 \quad \Rightarrow \quad 7a_2 = 7a_1 - 3a_1$

$\Rightarrow a_2 = \frac{4}{7} a_1$

$\frac{a_3}{8} = \frac{6 - a_1 - a_3}{6} \quad \Rightarrow \quad 7a_3 = 24 - 4a_1 \quad \Rightarrow \quad 7a_3 = 7a_1 - 4a_1 \quad \Rightarrow \quad a_3 = \frac{3}{7} a_1$

Thus $a_2 + a_3 = a_1$.

Similarly, we have $a_4 + a_5 = a_2$ and $a_6 + a_7 = a_3$.

The perimeter is P and

$P = 4(a_1 + a_2 + a_3 + a_4 + a_5 + a_6 + a_7)$
$= 4(a_1 + a_2 + a_3 + a_2 + a_3)$
$= 4(a_1 + a_1 + a_1) = 12a_1$
$= 12 \times \frac{24}{7} = \frac{288}{7}$.

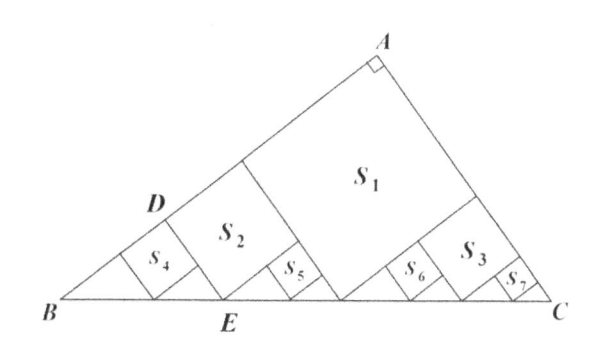

Twenty Mathcounts Target Round Tests — Test 7

MATHCOUNTS

■ **Mock Competition Seven** ■

Target Round

Name _____

State _____

DO NOT BEGIN UNTIL YOU ARE INSTRUCTED TO DO SO.

This section of the competition consists of eight problems, which will be presented in pairs. Work on one pair of problems will be completed and answers will be collected before the next pair is distributed. The time limit for each pair of problems is six minutes. The first pair of problems is on the other side of this sheet. When told to do so, turn the page over and begin working. Record only final answers in the designated blanks on the problem sheet. All answers must be complete, legible, and simplified to lowest terms. This round assumes the use of calculators, and calculations may also be done on scratch paper, but no other aids are allowed. If you complete the problems before time is called, use the time remaining to check your answers.

Total Correct	Scorer's Initials

Copyright MYMATHCOUNTS.COM. All rights reserved.

Twenty Mathcounts Target Round Tests **Test 7**

1. _____ The diameter $\overline{AB}$ of the circle in the diagram is trisected such that $AC = CD = DB$. Semicircles are determined by $\overline{AC}$, $\overline{AD}$, $\overline{CB}$, and $\overline{DB}$. What fractional portion of the large circle is the shaded area?

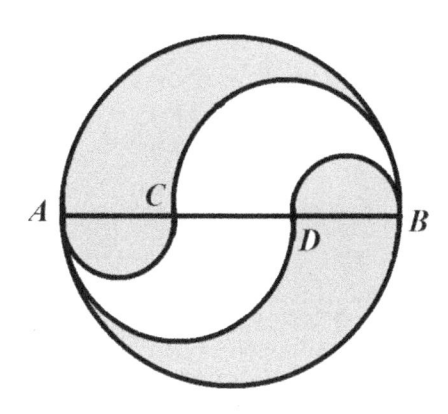

2. _____ What is the sum of the distinct prime numbers which divide $117^4 + 234^4$?

Twenty Mathcounts Target Round Tests   **Test 7**

3. _____ A closed cardboard box is twice as wide and five times as long as it is deep. If the total surface area is $416\frac{1}{2}$ square feet, then how many feet are in the sum of the length, width, and depth of the box?

4. _____ Each face of a cube is assigned a different even integer. Then each vertex is assigned the sum of the integer values on the faces that meet at the vertex. Finally, the vertex numbers are added. What is the largest number that must divide the final sum for every possible numbering of the faces?

Twenty Mathcounts Target Round Tests   **Test 7**

5. _____ Two squares on a 3 by 5 rectangular grid of 1-inch squares are randomly selected. What is the probability that the two squares are in either the same row or the same column? Express your answer as a common fraction.

6. _____ The multiples of 3 are arranged in the following manner:

Column 1	Column 2	Column 3	Column 4
3	6	9	12
21	18	15	12
21	24	27	30
39	36	33	30
39	42	...	...

In which column will the number 2013 appear?

57

7. _____ Erin's age on her birthday in 2014 is equal to the sum of the digits of her birth year. Danny's age, who is Erin's uncle, on his birthday in 2014 is also equal to the sum of the digits of his birth year. What will the sum of their birth years?

8. _____ How many isosceles triangles can be created on this 2 × 5 geoboard?

Twenty Mathcounts Target Round Tests Test 7

SOLUTIONS:

Problem 1: Solution: 2/3.

Since we look for the ratio of the areas, we can assign the values for $AC = 2$ and we label the areas as shown in the figure.

We like to find $\dfrac{2(x+z)}{2(x+y+z)} = \dfrac{x+z}{x+y+z}$.

We know that $x + y + z$ is half circle with the radius $6/2 = 3$.

So $x + y + z = \pi \times 3^2/2$.

$z = \pi \times 3^2/2 - (x + y) = \pi \times 3^2/2 - \pi \times 2^2/2 = \pi \times 5/2$.

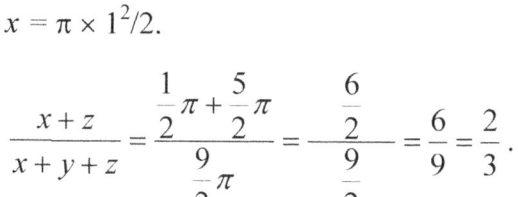

$x = \pi \times 1^2/2$.

$$\dfrac{x+z}{x+y+z} = \dfrac{\frac{1}{2}\pi + \frac{5}{2}\pi}{\frac{9}{2}\pi} = \dfrac{\frac{6}{2}}{\frac{9}{2}} = \dfrac{6}{9} = \dfrac{2}{3}.$$

Problem 2: Solution: 33.

$117^4 + 234^4 = 117^4 (1 + 2^4) = 117^4 \times 17$.

$117 = 3^2 \times 13$ and 17 is a prime numbers. So the sum is $3 + 13 + 17 = 33$.

Problem 3: Solution: 28.

Let the depth of the box be x.

The length will be $5x$ and the width will be $2x$.

The surface area will be $2(x \times 5x + 5x \times 2x + 2x \times x) = 416\dfrac{1}{2}$, or

$$2 \times 17x^2 = \dfrac{833}{2} \quad \Rightarrow \quad x^2 = \dfrac{49}{4} \quad \Rightarrow \quad x = \dfrac{7}{2}.$$

The sum of the length, width, and depth of the box is: $x + 5x + 2x = 8x = 8 \times \dfrac{7}{2} = 28$.

Problem 4: Solution: 8.

Let the six numbers on six faces be $2a$, $2b$, $2c$, $2d$, $2e$, $2f$, respectively. a, b, c, d, e, and f are any positive integers. Since each face has four vertices, each number on that face is added four times. So the final sum obtained by adding the vertex numbers is:

$4(2a+2b+2c+2d+2e+2f) = 8(a+b+c+d+e+f)$.

The largest number that must divide the final sum for every possible numbering of the faces is 8.

Problem 5: Solution: 3/7.

Method 1:

No matter how we select the first square (marked with "X"), we are always able to select one of the six squares (marked with "Δ") so that the two squares selected will be in either the same row or the same column, as shown in the figure below.

Thus the probability is $P = \dfrac{\binom{15}{1} \times \binom{6}{1}}{\binom{15}{1} \times \binom{14}{1}} = \dfrac{15 \times 6}{15 \times 14} = \dfrac{3}{7}$.

Method 2:

After we select one square (marked with "X"), we have 6 (marked with "Δ") out of 14 (total number of squares except the square marked with "X") chance to match it.

Thus the probability is $P = 1 \times \dfrac{6}{14} = \dfrac{3}{7}$.

Problem 6. Solution: 3rd column.

The arrangement is the same as the following one:

Column 1	Column 2	Column 3	Column 4
3	6	9	12
	18	15	
21	24	27	30
	36	33	
39	42	...	...

The pattern repeats every six numbers.

2013 is 2013/3 = 671st number in the list of multiples of 3 in order from the smallest to the greatest.

$671 = 111 \times 6 + 5$.

Thus 2013 is in the same column as the 5th number, which is 15, appearing in column 3.

Problem 7: Solution: 3994.

Let one of the two people's birth year be $\overline{19ab}$, where a and b are digits less than from 0 to 9.

$2014 - \overline{19ab} = 1 + 9 + a + b \Rightarrow 2014 - 1900 - 10a - b = 10 + a + b \Rightarrow 11a + 2b = 104$

a must be even and can be 8, 6, 4, 2, 0.

If $a = 8$, we have $11 \times 8 + 2b = 104 \Rightarrow b = 8$.

If $a = 6$, we have $11 \times 6 + 2b = 104 \Rightarrow b = 19$ (ignored since b is less than 10).

There is no other valid values of a.

Thus this person's birth year is 1988 and he must be Danny.

Let Erin's birth year be $\overline{20xy}$, where x and y are digits less than from 0 to 9.

$2014 - \overline{20xy} = 2 + 0 + x + y \Rightarrow 2014 - 2000 - 10x - y = 2 + x + y \Rightarrow 11x + 2y = 12$

x must be even and can only be 0. Then we have $11 \times 0 + 2y = 12 \Rightarrow y = 6$.

Thus Erin's birth year is 2006.

The sum of their birth years is $1988 + 2006 = 3994$.

Problem 8: Solution:.

We see four isosceles triangles for every four points arranged as follows:

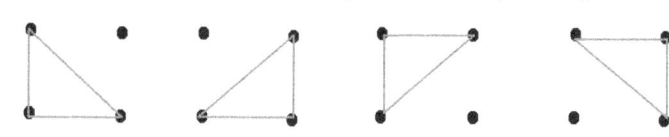

So we have $4 \times 4 = 16$ such isosceles triangles.

We have $3 \times 2 = 6$ isosceles triangles as shown in the figure below:

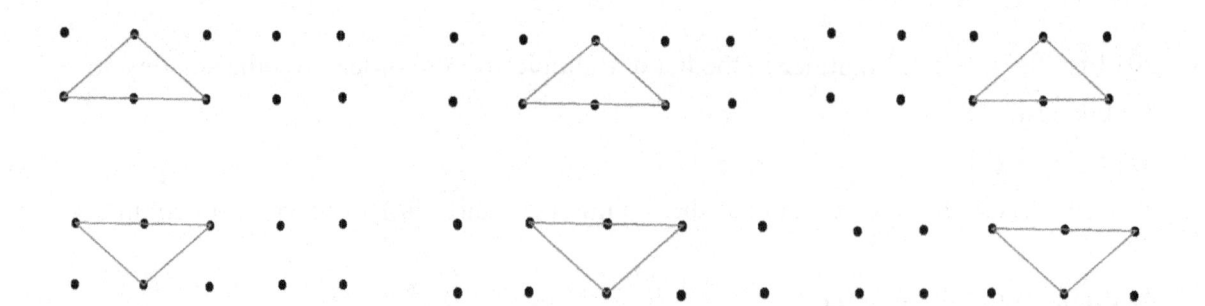

Twenty Mathcounts Target Round Tests   **Test 7**

We have $1 \times 2 = 2$ such isosceles triangles as shown in the figure below:

Total we have $16 + 6 + 2 = 24$ isosceles triangles

Twenty Mathcounts Target Round Tests Test 8

MATHCOUNTS

■ **Mock Competition Eight** ■

Target Round

Name _____

State _____

DO NOT BEGIN UNTIL YOU ARE INSTRUCTED TO DO SO.

This section of the competition consists of eight problems, which will be presented in pairs. Work on one pair of problems will be completed and answers will be collected before the next pair is distributed. The time limit for each pair of problems is six minutes. The first pair of problems is on the other side of this sheet. When told to do so, turn the page over and begin working. Record only final answers in the designated blanks on the problem sheet. All answers must be complete, legible, and simplified to lowest terms. This round assumes the use of calculators, and calculations may also be done on scratch paper, but no other aids are allowed. If you complete the problems before time is called, use the time remaining to check your answers.

Total Correct	Scorer's Initials

Copyright   MYMATHCOUNTS.COM. All rights reserved.

Twenty Mathcounts Target Round Tests — Test 8

1. _____ k is a positive integer. $k/2$ is a positive integer. $k/3$ is a square number. $k/5$ is a cubic number. What is the quotient when the smallest value of k is divided by 10000?

2. _____ Three points $A(0, 3)$, $B(6,3)$, $C(8,1)$ are on a circle. The figure shows a section of the arc of the circle. Find the coordinates of the center of the circle.

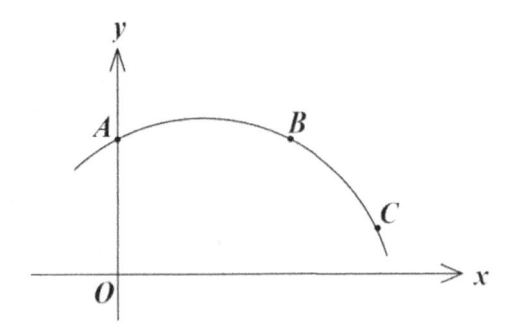

3. _____ Given fraction $\dfrac{k}{95+k}$, where $k = 1, 2, 3, \ldots, 2015$. How many of these 2015 fractions are in the simplest forms?

4. _____ If a 7-digit number $13xy26z$ is divisible by 264, find the greatest possible value of $x + y$.

5. _____ For real numbers a, b, c, if $a + b + c = 0$ and $a^2 + b^2 + c^2 = 294$, what is the greatest value for b?

6. _____ As shown in the figure, $AB = 8$. Two half circles are drawn inside the rectangle $ABCD$ using AB, and CD as the diameters, respectively. Using the two intersection points of two half circles as the diameter to draw another circle. This circle is exactly tangent to AB and CD. Find the sum of two shaded areas.

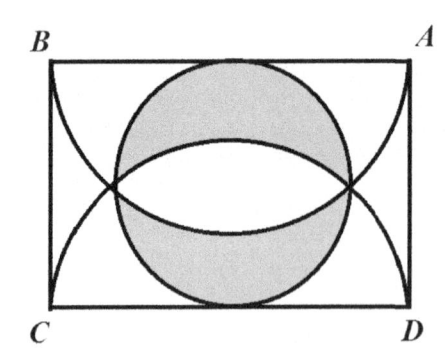

Twenty Mathcounts Target Round Tests Test 8

7. _____ There are two types of questions in a test: easy and hard. If you answer a hard question, you get 7 points for the correct answer and zero point for the wrong answer. If you answer an easy question, you get 4 points for the correct answer and 3 points deduction for the wrong answer. Alex answers correctly 15 questions and gets 48 points. How many easy questions are there in the test?

8. _____ As shown in the figure, parallelogram $ABCD$. M and N are midpoints of BC and CD, respectively. $AN = 2$, $AM = 4$. $\angle MAN = 60°$. Find AD.

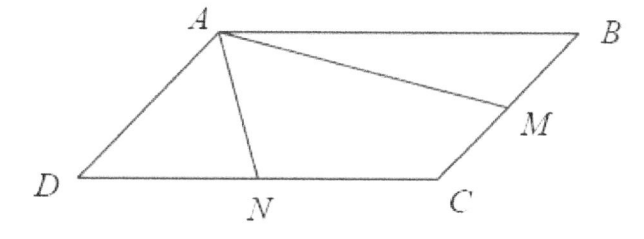

SOLUTIONS:

Problem 1: Solution: 108.
Let $k = 2a = 3b^2 = 5c^3$.
Since we want the smallest value of k, we let $c = 2 \times 3 \times 5$ first.
Then we have $k = 5 \times 2^3 \times 3^3 \times 5^3$ that is not a square number when divided by 3.
If $c = 2^2 \times 3 \times 5$, $k = 2^6 \times 3^3 \times 5^4 = 1080000$.
So the number when the smallest value of k is divided by 10000 is 1080000/10000 = 108.

Problem 2: Solution: (3, −2).
Connect AB. The coordinate of the midpoint of AB is (3, 3). The center of the circle must be on the line $x = 3$. Let the coordinate of the center O be (3, t).
$\overline{DB}^2 = \overline{DC}^2 \Rightarrow (3-6)^2 + (t-3)^2 = (3-8)^2 + (t-1)^2 \Rightarrow$
$t = -2$.
The coordinate of the center is (3, −2).

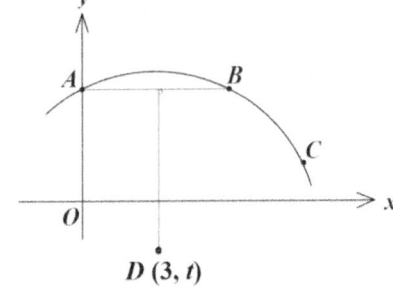

Problem 3: Solution: 1527.
$\dfrac{k}{95+k} = \dfrac{k}{5 \times 19 + k}$.

When k is a multiple of 5 or 19, the fraction is reducible and is not in the simplest forms.
$2015 - [\dfrac{2015}{5}] - [\dfrac{2015}{19}] + [\dfrac{2015}{95}] = 2015 - 403 - 106 + 21 = 1527$.

Problem 4: Solution: 14.
$264 = 8 \times 3 \times 11$. So $26z$ must be a multiple of 8. Thus $z = 4$.
We know that $13xy4264$ is divisible by 11. Thus we have $4 + 2 + x + 1 - (6 + y + 3) = x - y + 3$ which is divisible by 11.
So we have $x - y - 2 = 0$, or $x = y + 2$ \hfill (1)
(Note that (i) $x - y - 2 = 11$ is not possible since x and y are digits, and (ii) $x > y$).
We also know that $13xy264$ is divisible by 3.
Thus we have $1 + 3 + x + y + 2 + 6 + 4 = x + y + 15 + 1$ which is divisible by 3, or $x + y + 1$ is divisible by 3.

Considering (1), we have $x + y + 1 = 2y + 3$ is divisible by 3, or $2y$ is divisible by 3.
Since $y < x$, $y = 3$ or 6 (not 9).
We know that $x = y + 2$. So we have $x = 5$ or $x = 8$.
$x + y = 8 + 6 = 14$ or $x + y = 5 + 3 = 8$.
The answer is 14. (Two numbers are 1353264 and 1386264).

Problem 5: Solution: 14.
Let $c = -a - b$.
$a^2 + b^2 + (-a-b)^2 = 294 \implies 2a^2 + 2ab + 2b^2 - 294 = 0 \implies a^2 + ab + b^2 - 147 = 0$.
This is a quadratic equation about a.
Since a, b, c are real, $\Delta = b^2 - 4(b^2 - 147) \geq 0$.
$-3b^2 + 588 \geq 0 \implies b^2 - 196 \leq 0 \implies b^2 \leq 196$.
$-14 \leq a \leq 14$.
The greatest value is 14.

Problem 6: Solution: 16.

We label the figure as follows. Connect EF, OF. $OE = OF = \frac{1}{2}GE = r$.

$EF = FD = \frac{1}{2}CD = \frac{1}{2} \times 8 = 4$.

Applying Pythagorean Theorem to right triangle OEF:
$r^2 + r^2 = 4^2 \implies r = 2\sqrt{2}$.

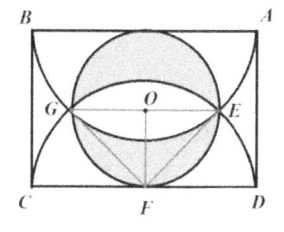

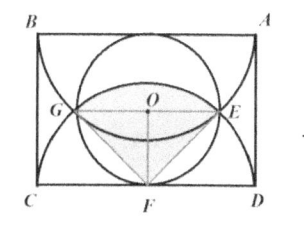

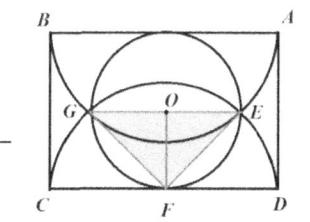

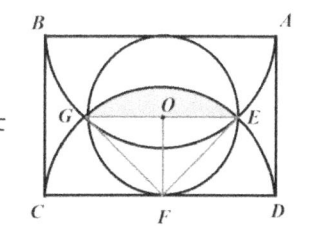

From the figure, we have $\pi \times 4^2 \times \frac{90°}{360°} - \frac{4\sqrt{2} \times 2\sqrt{2}}{2} = 4\pi - 8$.

The answer is $\pi \times (2\sqrt{2})^2 - 2(4\pi - 8) = 16$.

Twenty Mathcounts Target Round Tests　　　　　　　　　　　Test 8

Problem 7: Solution: 19.

Let the number of hard questions be h, the number of easy question Alex answered correctly be e_c, and the number of easy question Alex answered wrong be e_w.

$$\begin{cases} 7h + 4e_c - 3e_w = 48 & (1) \\ h + e_c = 15 & (2) \end{cases}$$

We write (2) as $h = 15 - e_c$ 　　　　　　　　　　　　　　　　　　　(3)

Substituting (3) into (1):

$7(15 - e_c) + 4e_c - 3e_w = 48$ ⇒ $105 - 7e_c + 4e_c - 3e_w = 48$ ⇒ $105 - 3e_c - 3e_w = 48$ ⇒ $105 - 48 = 3(e_c + e_w)$ ⇒ $e_c + e_w = 19$.

Problem 8: Solution: $\dfrac{8}{3}$.

Method 1:

Let E be the midpoint of AM. Connect EN. Connect MN. $\overline{AE} = \overline{EM} = 2$.

We know that $\angle MAN = 60°$. So $\triangle ANE$ is an equilateral triangle and $\overline{EN} = 2$.

Let $\overline{AD} = x$. Then $\overline{MC} = \dfrac{x}{2}$. So EN is the midline of trapezoid $ADCM$.

$\dfrac{x + \dfrac{x}{2}}{2} = 2$ ⇒ $x = \dfrac{8}{3} = \overline{AD}$.

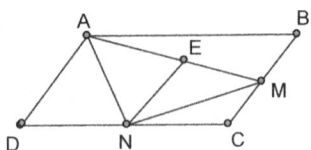

Method 2:

Extend AN and BC to meet at E. We see that $\angle AND = \angle ENC$ (vertical angles), $\angle ADN = \angle ECN$ (alternate interior angles of parallel lines AD and CE).

$DN = NC$.

Thus $\triangle AND$ is congruent to $\triangle ENC$. $AD = EC$.

$AN = NE = 2$. So $AE = 2 + 2 = 4 = AM$.

$\triangle AEM$ is an isosceles triangle with $AE = AM$.

We are given that $\angle EAM = 60°$. So $\angle AEM = \angle AME = 60°$. Thus $\triangle AEM$ is an equilateral triangle and $EM = 4 = EC + CM = AD + \dfrac{1}{2}AD$ ⇒ $\dfrac{3}{2}AD = 4$ ⇒ $AD = \dfrac{8}{3}$.

Twenty Mathcounts Target Round Tests — Test 9

MATHCOUNTS

■ Mock Competition Nine ■

Target Round

Name _____

State _____

DO NOT BEGIN UNTIL YOU ARE INSTRUCTED TO DO SO.

This section of the competition consists of eight problems, which will be presented in pairs. Work on one pair of problems will be completed and answers will be collected before the next pair is distributed. The time limit for each pair of problems is six minutes. The first pair of problems is on the other side of this sheet. When told to do so, turn the page over and begin working. Record only final answers in the designated blanks on the problem sheet. All answers must be complete, legible, and simplified to lowest terms. This round assumes the use of calculators, and calculations may also be done on scratch paper, but no other aids are allowed. If you complete the problems before time is called, use the time remaining to check your answers.

Total Correct	Scorer's Initials

Copyright   MYMATHCOUNTS.COM. All rights reserved.

Twenty Mathcounts Target Round Tests — Test 9

1. _____ Suppose the function f satisfies the following:

(a) $f(n) > 0$ for all integers n,
(b) $f(n) = [f(n-1)]^2$, and
(c) $f(4) = 625$.

Find $f(1)$.

2. _____ Eight congruent circles are arranged in the pattern shown such that each circle is tangent to one or more circles. What is the sum of the shaded areas if the radius of each circle is 1?

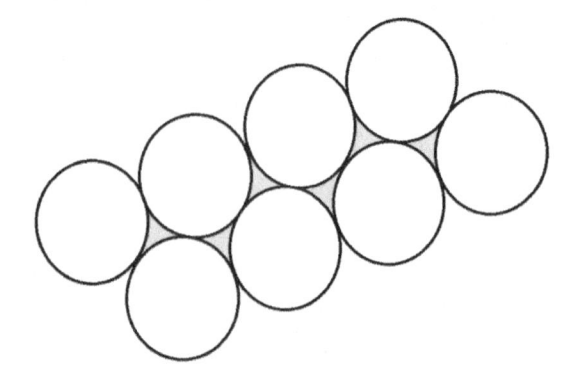

Twenty Mathcounts Target Round Tests　　　　　　　　　　　　　　　Test 9

3. _____ Bob's running shoes had 1 inch of tread when new. He has run 540 miles in the shoes and has $\frac{4}{9}$ inches of tread left. Assuming the tread wears at a constant rate, how many more miles can Bob run before his shoes have no tread left?

4. _____ In the set of real numbers, given $a > 0$ find the fraction between $-\frac{1}{3}a$ and $-\frac{2}{5}a$ which is three times as far from the smaller as to the larger fraction. Express your answer in terms of a.

5. _____ How many cubic units are in the volume of the solid created by rotating the quadrilateral whose vertices are (0, 4), (6, 4), (6, 2), and (0, 0) around the y-axis? Express your answer in terms of π.

6. _____ What is the value of the largest mean among the following sets of whole numbers?

A: all multiples of 3 from 1 to 100, inclusive,
B: all multiples of 4 from 1 to 100, inclusive,
C: all multiples of 6 from 1 to 100, inclusive,
D: all multiples of 7 from 1 to 100, inclusive,
E: all multiples of 9 from 1 to 100, inclusive.

7. _____ Given $DC = 15$, $CB = \frac{1}{3}AD$, $AB = \frac{1}{4}AD$, and $ED = \frac{4}{9}AD$, find GB.

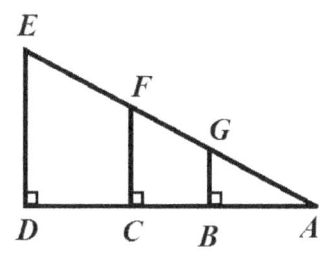

8. _____ A circular sheet of paper with a radius of 15 cm is cut into three congruent sectors. What is the height of the cone in centimeters that can be created by rolling one of the sections until the edges meet? Express your answer in simplest radical form.

Twenty Mathcounts Target Round Tests Test 9

SOLUTIONS:

Problem 1: $\sqrt{5}$.

$f(n) = [f(n-1)]^2 \Rightarrow f(4) = [f(4-1)]^2 \Rightarrow 625 = [f(3)]^2$

Since $f(n) > 0$ for all integers n, $f(3) = 25$.

$f(3) = [f(3-1)]^2 \Rightarrow 25 = [f(2)]^2 \Rightarrow f(2) = 5$.
$f(2) = [f(2-1)]^2 \Rightarrow 5 = [f(1)]^2 \Rightarrow f(1) = \sqrt{5}$.

Problem 2: Solution: $6\sqrt{3} - 3\pi$.

We connect the centers of three circles. ABC is an equilateral triangle.

The area of the triangle is $\frac{1}{4}a^2\sqrt{3} = \frac{1}{4} \times 2^2\sqrt{3} = \sqrt{3}$.

The shaded area is $\sqrt{3} - \frac{1}{6} \times \pi \times 1^2 \times 3 = \sqrt{3} - \frac{1}{2}\pi$.

The answer is $6(\sqrt{3} - \frac{1}{2}\pi) = 6\sqrt{3} - 3\pi$.

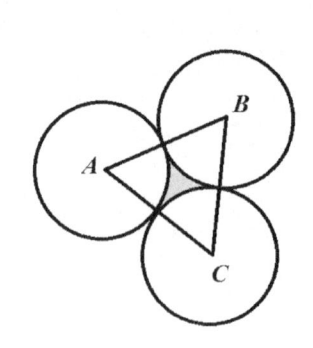

Problem 3: Solution: 432 miles.

We know that Bob runs 540 miles with $1 \times \frac{5}{9} = \frac{5}{9}$ inches tread.

Let x be the number of miles wearing $\frac{4}{9}$ inches tread. Using proportion, we have

$\dfrac{540}{\frac{5}{9}} = \dfrac{x}{\frac{4}{9}} \Rightarrow \dfrac{540}{5} = \dfrac{x}{4} \Rightarrow 108 = \dfrac{x}{4} \Rightarrow x = 432$.

Problem 4: Solution: $-\dfrac{7}{20}a$.

We know that $a > 0$, $-\dfrac{1}{3}a > -\dfrac{2}{5}a$.

Let the fraction be m.

We label the numbers as shown in the figure.

76

$$-\frac{1}{3}a - (-\frac{2}{5}a) = 4x \Rightarrow \quad 4x = \frac{1}{15}a \Rightarrow \quad x = \frac{1}{60}a$$

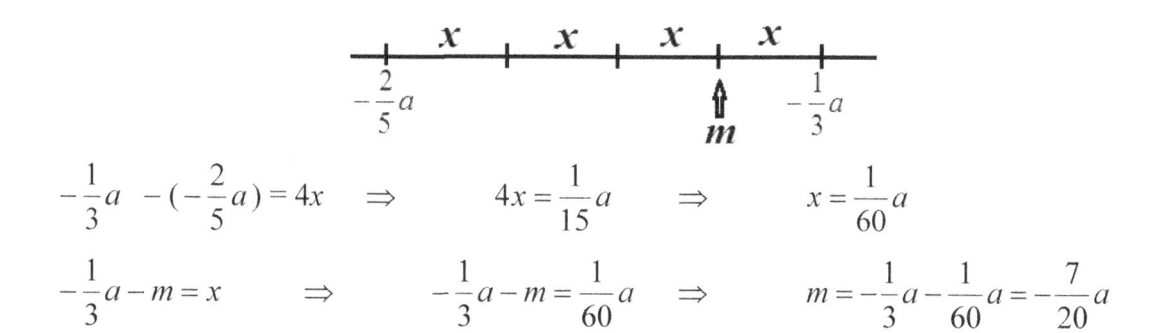

$$-\frac{1}{3}a - m = x \Rightarrow \quad -\frac{1}{3}a - m = \frac{1}{60}a \Rightarrow \quad m = -\frac{1}{3}a - \frac{1}{60}a = -\frac{7}{20}a$$

Problem 5: Solution: 96π.

We draw the figure of the quadrilateral as shown:

The solid figure after rotation is shown as follows:

The volume of the solid consists of two parts: a cylinder with radius 6 and height 2, and a cone with the radius 6 and the height 2:

$$\pi \times 6^2 \times 2 + \frac{\pi \times 6^2 \times 2}{3} = \frac{4\pi \times 6^2 \times 2}{3} = 96\pi.$$

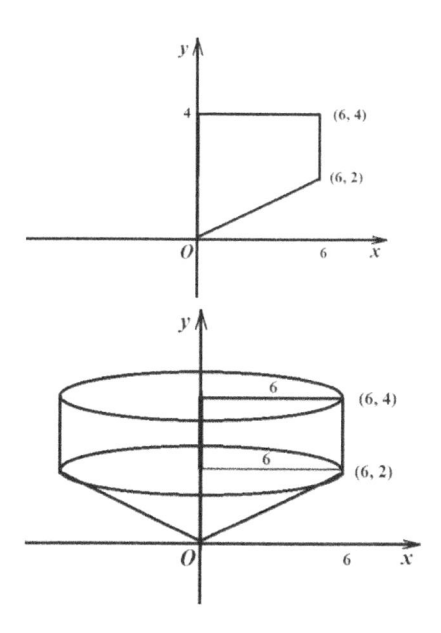

Problem 6. Solution: 54.

The mean of all whole numbers of multiples of 3:
$$\frac{(3+99) \times 33}{2 \times 33} = \frac{(3+99)}{2} = 51.$$

The mean of all whole numbers of multiples of 4:
$$\frac{4+100}{2} = 52.$$

The mean of all whole numbers of multiples of 6:
$$\frac{6+96}{2} = 51.$$

The mean of all whole numbers of multiples of 7:

$\dfrac{7+98}{2} = 52.5$.

The mean of all whole numbers of multiples of 9:

$\dfrac{9+99}{2} = 54$.

The greatest value is 54.

Problem 7: Solution: 4.

We know that $DC + CB + AB = AD$.

So $AD = 15 + \dfrac{1}{3}AD + \dfrac{1}{4}AD \quad \Rightarrow \quad \dfrac{5}{12}AD = 15 \quad \Rightarrow \quad AD = 36$

Thus $CB = \dfrac{1}{3}AD = 12$, $AB = \dfrac{1}{4}AD = 9$, and $ED = \dfrac{4}{9}AD = 16$.

$\triangle AED \sim \triangle AGB$.

$\dfrac{ED}{GB} = \dfrac{AD}{AB} \quad \Rightarrow \quad GB = \dfrac{ED \times AB}{AD} = \dfrac{16 \times 9}{36} = 4$.

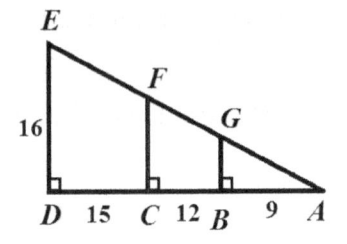

Problem 8: Solution: $10\sqrt{2}$.

The circumference of the circle is $2\pi \times 15 = 30\pi$.

One third of it is $30\pi/3 = 10\pi$. By Pythagorean Theorem, $h = \sqrt{15^2 - 5^2} = 10\sqrt{2}$.

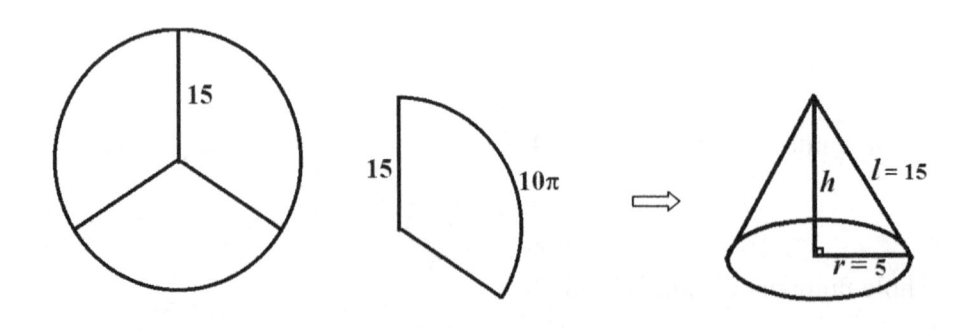

Twenty Mathcounts Target Round Tests **Test 10**

MATHCOUNTS

■ **Mock Competition Ten** ■

Target Round

Name _____

State _____

DO NOT BEGIN UNTIL YOU ARE INSTRUCTED TO DO SO.

This section of the competition consists of eight problems, which will be presented in pairs. Work on one pair of problems will be completed and answers will be collected before the next pair is distributed. The time limit for each pair of problems is six minutes. The first pair of problems is on the other side of this sheet. When told to do so, turn the page over and begin working. Record only final answers in the designated blanks on the problem sheet. All answers must be complete, legible, and simplified to lowest terms. This round assumes the use of calculators, and calculations may also be done on scratch paper, but no other aids are allowed. If you complete the problems before time is called, use the time remaining to check your answers.

Total Correct	Scorer's Initials

Copyright   MYMATHCOUNTS.COM. All rights reserved.

Twenty Mathcounts Target Round Tests   **Test 10**

1. _____ a and b are positive integers and $a > b$. If $ab - 2a - b = 17$, find a.

2. _____ As shown in the figure, $ABCD$ is a rectangle with $\overline{AB} = 72$, $\overline{BC} = 96$. M is on $\overline{AD}$. N is on $\overline{CD}$. $\overline{MN}$ is the crease. D is exactly overlapping with E that is the midpoint of $\overline{BC}$. Find $\overline{MN}$.

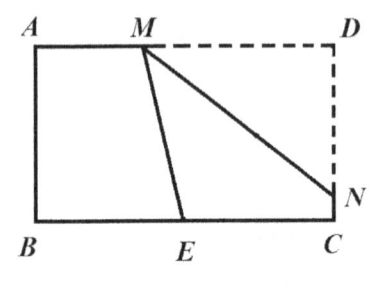

3. _____ As shown in the figure, $ABCD$ is a trapezoid. $\angle ABC = 90°$, $\overline{AD} = 6$, $\overline{BC} = 12$. If a circle is inscribed in $ABCD$, find $\overline{CD}$.

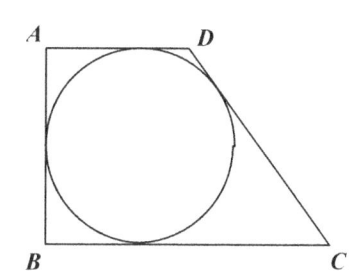

4. _____ Distribute 2015 marbles to n people. Each person gets a different number of marbles and each person gets at least one marble. Find the greatest possible value for n.

5. _____ A four-digit number *aabb* is a square number and both *a* and *b* are positive integers less than 10. What is the value for *a*?

6. _____ Put a positive integer *N* to the right side of any positive integer resulting a new number (for example, add 5 to the right side of 92 resulting 925). If the resulting number is divisible by *N*, then *N* is called a "magic number". How many "magic numbers" are there less than 2015?

7. _____ Alex and his five friends were at his farm to pick up some oranges. The number of oranges each person picked is different. Total they had 800 oranges. Bob and Charles got less number of oranges than other people. At most how many oranges did Bob and Charles pick together?

8. _____ Alex, Bob, Charles, and Danny play a chess tournament. Each person plays exactly one game against every other player. The winner of a game gets 3 points and the loser gets zero point. For a tie, each player gets 1 point. After the tournament, each person gets a different number of points that can form exactly an arithmetic sequence with the common difference of 1. What is the sum of the points of all players?

Twenty Mathcounts Target Round Tests — Test 10

SOLUTIONS:

Problem 1: Solution: 20.
$a(b-2)-(b-2)=17+2 \Rightarrow (b-2)(a-1)=19$
We know that $a>b$. So $a-1>b-2$
We have $a-1=19$ and $b-2=1$.
$a=20, b=3$.

Problem 2: Solution: $26\sqrt{13}$.

Method 1:
Let $\overline{CN}=x \Rightarrow \overline{EN}=\overline{ND}=72-x$. $\overline{EC}=96\div 2=48$
Applying Pythagorean Theorem to right triangle ECN:
$48^2+x^2=(72-x)^2 \Rightarrow x=20$. So
$\overline{EN}=72-20=52$.
Draw $\overline{MF}\perp\overline{BC}$ at F. Then $\overline{MF}=72$.

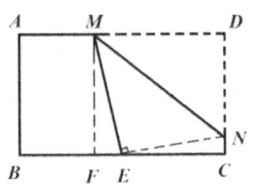

We also see that $\angle MEF+\angle NEC=90°=\angle NEC+\angle ENC \Rightarrow \angle MEF=\angle ENC$
$\angle MFE=\angle C=90°$.
Thus $\triangle MFE\sim\triangle ECN$.
$\dfrac{\overline{ME}}{\overline{EN}}=\dfrac{\overline{MF}}{\overline{EC}} \Rightarrow \dfrac{\overline{ME}}{52}=\dfrac{72}{48} \Rightarrow \overline{ME}=78$

$\overline{MN}=\sqrt{78^2+52^2}=26\sqrt{13}$.

Method 2:
Applying Pythagorean Theorem to right triangle ECN:
$48^2+x^2=(72-x)^2 \Rightarrow x=20$. So
$\overline{DN}=72-20=52$.
Connect ED.
Applying Pythagorean Theorem to right triangle ECD:
$72^2+48^2=ED^2 \Rightarrow ED=24\sqrt{13}$. So $FD=12\sqrt{13}$.

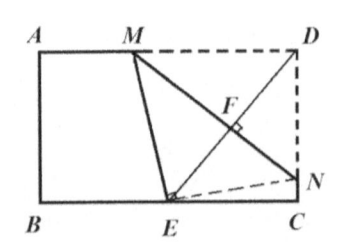

Twenty Mathcounts Target Round Tests   **Test 10**

Applying Pythagorean Theorem to right triangle *DFN*:

$DN^2 - FN^2 = DF^2 \implies FN = \sqrt{52^2 - (12\sqrt{13})^2} = 8\sqrt{13}$.

We know that $DN^2 = MN \times FN \implies MN = \dfrac{DN^2}{FN} = \dfrac{52^2}{8\sqrt{13}} = 26\sqrt{13}$.

Problem 3: Solution: 10.

Draw $\overline{DE} \perp \overline{BC}$ at *E*.

Let $\overline{AB} = \overline{DE} = a, \overline{CD} = b, \overline{CE} = 12 - 6 = 6$.

We know that $\overline{AB} + \overline{CD} = \overline{AD} + \overline{BC}$.

So $a + b = 6 + 12 = 18$ (1)

        $a^2 + 6^2 = b^2$ (2)

(1) can be written as: $a = 18 - b$ (3)

Substituting (3) into (2): $(18 - b)^2 + 36 = b^2 \implies b = 10$.

The answer is $\overline{CD} = 10$.

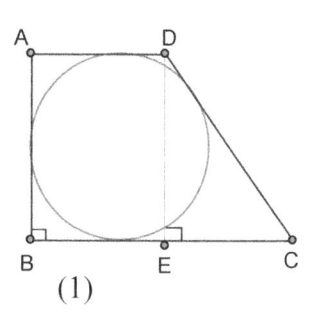

Problem 4: Solution: 62.

We distribute the marbles to *n* people this way:

First person gets 1 marble, second person gets 2 marbles, third person gets 3 marbles,…, and *n*th person gets *n* marbles.

After that, we have *m* < *n* marbles left. We give these *m* marbles to the *n*th person. So everyone gets a different number of marbles.

$1 + 2 + 3 + \cdots + n \le 2015 \implies \dfrac{(1+n)n}{2} \le 2015 \implies (1+n)n \le 4030$.

$\sqrt{4030} < 64$. So we test $n = 63$ and 62: $\dfrac{(1+62)62}{2} = 1953 < 2015 < \dfrac{(1+63)63}{2} \le 2016$.

The greatest value of *n* is 62.

Problem 5: Solution: 7.

Method 1:

$\overline{aabb} = 100\overline{aa} + \overline{bb} = 11(100a + b)$.

Since $\overline{aabb}$ is a square number, $(100a + b)$ must be divisible by 11.

Since $100a + b = 11 \times 9a + a + b$, $a + b$ is also a multiple of 11. The only value for the sum is $a + b = 11$.
We can write $100a + b = 99a + 11 = 11(9a + 1)$
We see that $9a + 1$ must be a square number. So $a = 7$.

Method 2:
When the units digit of a square number is odd, its tens digit must be even.
The last digit of a square number can only be 0, 1, 4, 5, 6, or 9. So b can only be 4 or 6.
When the units digit of a square number is 6, its tens digit must be odd. So b can only be 4.
Since $(a + b) - (a + b) = 0$, $\overline{aabb}$ must divisible by 11.
Since $\overline{aabb}$ is a square number, it must be divisible by $11^2 = 121$.
We use the calculator to do the calculations:
$\sqrt{9944}$, $\sqrt{8844}$, $\sqrt{7744}$, ..., $\sqrt{1144}$. Only $\sqrt{7744} = 88$ is an integer.
Therefore $a = 7$.

Problem 6: Solution: 15.
Let X be any positive integer.
Case 1: N is a single digit number. $\boxed{XN} = 10X + N$.
Since $10X + N$ is divisible by N, N must be a factor of 10. So $N = 1, 2,$ or 5.

Case 2: N is a 2-digit number. $\boxed{XN} = 100X + N$.
Since $100X + N$ is divisible by N, N must be a factor of 100. So $N = 10, 20, 25, 50$.

Case 3: N is a 3-digit number. $\boxed{XN} = 1000X + N$.
Since $1000X + N$ is divisible by N, N must be a factor of 1000. So $N = 100, 125, 200, 250, 500$.

Case 4: N is a 4-digit number. $\boxed{XN} = 10000X + N$.

Since $10000X + N$ is divisible by N, N must be a factor of 10000 and $N < 2015$. So $N = 1000, 1250, 2000$.

The answer is $3 + 4 + 5 + 3 = 15$.

Problem 7: Solution: 162.

Method 1:

Since nobody has the same number of oranges, let the first person get 1 orange, second person get 2, ..., and sixth person get 6.

$800 - (1 + 2 + 3 + 4 + 5 + 6) = 779$.

Then we distribute 779 oranges to 6 people: $779 \div 6 = 129$ R5.

We distribute 5 oranges left to five people (one person each).

At this moment, Bob got the least number of oranges ($1 + 129 = 130$) and Charles got $2 + 129 + 1 = 132$.

The answer is $130 + 132 = 162$.

Method 2:

Since we want the greatest possible values for Bob and Charles, we first distribute the oranges evenly and then we adjust:

$800/6 = 133$ R 2

$133, 133, 133, 133, 133, 135 \Rightarrow 131, 132, 133, 134, 135, 135 \Rightarrow 130, 132, 133, 134, 135, 136$.

The answer is $130 + 132 = 162$.

Problem 8: Solution: 14.

Method 1:

Let four people's scores be $x, x+1, x+2, x+3$.

$2 \times 6 \leq x + x + 1 + x + 2 + x + 3 \leq 3 \times 6$

$\dfrac{3}{2} \leq x \leq 3$

$x = 2$ or 3.

When $x = 3$, total scores are $3 + 4 + 5 + 6 = 18$. In this case, one of the four players must get 0 point.

So $x = 2$. When $x = 2$, total scores are $2 + 3 + 4 + 5 = 14$. This case works (for example, Alex: 5 points (win, tie, tie), Bob: 4 points (lose, win, tie), Charles: 3 points (tie, tie, tie); Danny: 2 points (tie, tie, lose).

Method 2:

The greatest score can be $3 \times 6 = 18$:

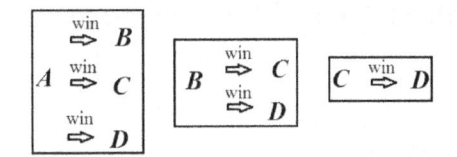

[Figure: A wins→B, A wins→C, A wins→D; B wins→C, B wins→D; C wins→D]

The least score can be $2 \times 6 = 12$:

[Figure: A tie→B, A tie→C, A tie→D; B tie→C, B tie→D; C tie→D]

$x + x + 1 + x + 2 + x + 3 = 4x + 6$. So $\dfrac{3}{2} \le x \le 3$. Since x is integer, $x = 2$ or 3.

When $x = 3$, the total score is 18.

$3w + t = 18$ \hfill (1)

$6 \ge w + t$ \hfill (2)

(1) + (2): $2w \ge 12$ $\Rightarrow$ $w \ge 6$, which contradicts to (2).

So the only value for x is 2. The following figure shows one of the cases working.

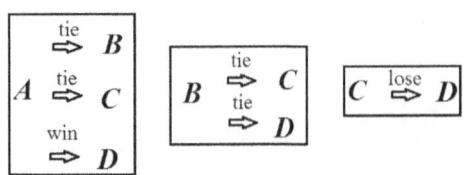

[Figure: A tie→B, A tie→C, A win→D; B tie→C, B tie→D; C lose→D]

Twenty Mathcounts Target Round Tests Test 11

MATHCOUNTS

■ Mock Competition Eleven ■

Target Round

Name _____

State _____

DO NOT BEGIN UNTIL YOU ARE INSTRUCTED TO DO SO.

This section of the competition consists of eight problems, which will be presented in pairs. Work on one pair of problems will be completed and answers will be collected before the next pair is distributed. The time limit for each pair of problems is six minutes. The first pair of problems is on the other side of this sheet. When told to do so, turn the page over and begin working. Record only final answers in the designated blanks on the problem sheet. All answers must be complete, legible, and simplified to lowest terms. This round assumes the use of calculators, and calculations may also be done on scratch paper, but no other aids are allowed. If you complete the problems before time is called, use the time remaining to check your answers.

Total Correct	Scorer's Initials

Copyright   MYMATHCOUNTS.COM. All rights reserved.

Twenty Mathcounts Target Round Tests   **Test 11**

1. _____ What is the smallest possible product of a four-digit number and a three-digit number obtained from seven distinct nonzero digits?

2. _____ Alex gave some pencils to each of his three sisters. He gave half of his pencils plus one more to Betsy. He then gave half of what he had left plus two more pencils to Catherine. Finally, he gave half of what he had left plus three more pencils to Daisy. He then had no pencils left. How many pencils did he originally have?

3. _____ In the triangle pictured, points B, R, S, and H are collinear, BR = 2.5(RS), and BR = 5(SH). To the nearest tenth, the area of quadrilateral ARCS is what percent of the area of triangle ABC?

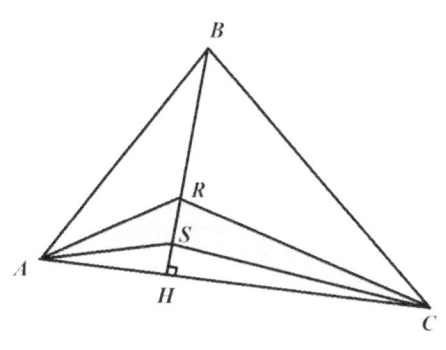

4. _____ At Sandy's Skateboard Shop, ten of the employees are to be rewarded by a trip to the skateboard expo in St. Louis, Missouri. Sandy likes each employee equally, so she decides to determine who will go by having the 20 employees stand equally spaced on the circumference of a circle and successively count off 1, 2, 3, 4, 5, 6, 1, 2, 3, 4, 5, 6, . . . , repeatedly. Each person who says '6' steps out of the circle and picks up a travel ticket. What is the number of degrees in the measure of the central acute angle between the second and last person who receives the trip?

Twenty Mathcounts Target Round Tests   **Test 11**

5. _____ Find the number of degrees in the positive difference between the sum of the measures of the five acute interior angles and the sum of the measures of the five obtuse exterior angles of the five-pointed star.

6. _____ General lighting standards for buildings dictate that rooms illuminated by circular light fixtures be designed so that the light from each circular lamp (as indicated in the diagram by the six dots) has a radius of light of 20 feet and the lamps are spaced $20\sqrt{2}$ feet apart. How many square feet are in the total area of overlap (marked "s" in the diagram)? Express your answer in terms of π.

Twenty Mathcounts Target Round Tests   **Test 11**

7. _____ The notation $a \equiv b \pmod{n}$ means $(a - b)$ is a multiple of n where n is a positive integer greater than one. Find the sum of all possible values of n such that both of the following are true: $567 \equiv 138 \pmod{n}$ and $366 \equiv 223 \pmod{n}$.

8. _____ A $5 \times 5 \times 5$ cube is made leaving a 3 cube by 3 cube by 5 cube hole in the interior. The figure is then dipped in paint. How many of the cubes are painted on exactly three faces?

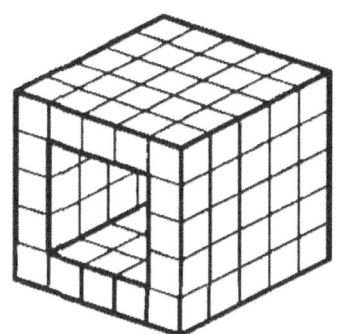

Twenty Mathcounts Target Round Tests Test 11

SOLUTIONS:

Problem 1: 333045.

We use smallest possible digits: 1, 2, 3, 4, 5, 6, 7, 8.

Put 1 and 2 this way:

1
2

Next we put the digits 3 and 4. The rule is that smaller number goes with smaller number and bigger number goes with bigger number (in our case, 3 goes with 1 and 4 goes with 4.

1	3
2	4

then we put 5 going with 13 and 6 with 24.

1	3	5
2	4	6

Then we have 7 left. So 7 needs to go with 246.

1	3	5	
2	4	6	7

The smallest possible product is then 333045.

Problem 2: Solution: 34.

We go backward.

Let x be the number of pencils Alex had before he gave to Daisy.

Twenty Mathcounts Target Round Tests   Test 11

$$x - (\frac{1}{2}x + 3) = 0 \quad \Rightarrow \quad x = 6.$$

Let y be the number of pencils Alex had before he gave to Catherine.

$$y - (\frac{1}{2}y + 2) = 6 \quad \Rightarrow \quad y = 16.$$

Let z be the number of pencils Alex had before he gave to Betsy.

$$z - (\frac{1}{2}z + 1) = 16 \quad \Rightarrow \quad z = 34.$$

The answer is 34.

Problem 3: Solution: 25%.

We know that $BR = 2.5(RS)$, and $BR = 5(SH)$. So $2.5(RS) = 5(SH)$, or $RS = 2SH$. Let $SH = x$. Then $BR = 5x$ and $RS = 2x$. From the figure we see that $\triangle ABR$, $\triangle ARS$, and $\triangle ASH$ are triangles with the same height. So the ratio of the areas is the same as the ratio of the lengths of bases.

$$\frac{S_{\triangle ARS}}{S_{\triangle ABH}} = \frac{2x}{5x + 2x + x} = \frac{S_{\triangle CRS}}{S_{\triangle CBH}} = \frac{S_{\triangle ARS} + S_{ARS}}{S_{\triangle ABH} + S_{ABH}} = \frac{2}{8} = \frac{1}{4} = 25\%.$$

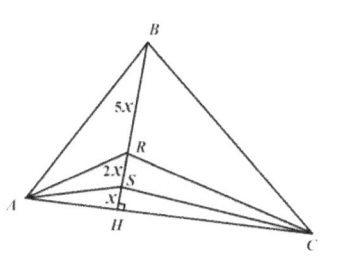

Problem 4: Solution: 36°.

We divide the circle by 20 numbers as shown in the figure. Each sector is 360/20 = 18°. The second person has the number 12 and the last person has the number 14. So the angle formed is 2 × 18 = 36°.

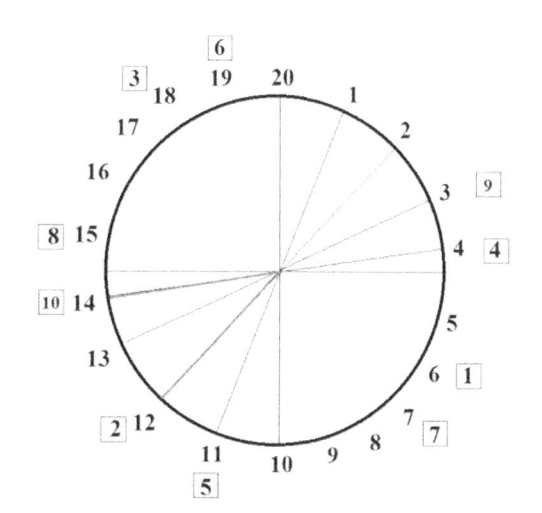

Twenty Mathcounts Target Round Tests   Test 11

Problem 5: Solution: 360°.

Method 1:

We connect $ABCDE$. We label each angle as shown in the figure.
We like to find $(x_1 + x_2 + x_3 + x_4 + x_5) - (a_2 + b_2 + c_2 + d_2 + e_2)$.
For the pentagon $ABCDE$, the sum of the inferior angles is $180(n-2) = 180(5-2) = 540°$, or

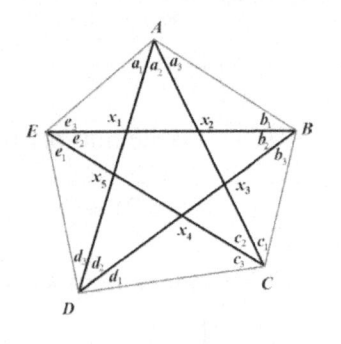

$$a_1 + a_2 + a_3 + b_1 + b_2 + b_3 + c_1 + c_2 + c_3 + d_1 + d_2 + d_3 + e_1 + e_2 + e_3 = 540 \qquad (1)$$

We also can write

$$a_1 + x_1 + e_3 + e_1 + x_5 + d_3 + d_1 + x_4 + c_3 + c_1 + x_3 + b_3 + b_1 + x_2 + a_3 = 5 \times 180 = 900 \qquad (2)$$

$(2) - (1)$: $(x_1 + x_2 + x_3 + x_4 + x_5) - (a_2 + b_2 + c_2 + d_2 + e_2) = 360$.

Method 2:

We label each angle as shown in the figure.
We like to find $(x_1 + x_2 + x_3 + x_4 + x_5) - (a + b + c + d + e)$.
For the pentagon shown below, the sum of the interior angles is $180(n-2) = 180(5-2) = 540°$.
That is $x_1 + x_2 + x_3 + x_4 + x_5 = 540$ (1)

We use the following relationship to solve our problem:
$\theta = \alpha + \beta + \gamma$.

$x_1 = a + c + e$ (2)
$x_2 = a + d + b$ (3)
$x_3 = c + e + b$ (4)
$x_4 = d + a + c$ (5)
$x_5 = e + b + d$ (6)

Adding 2) to (6) together we have
$x_1 + x_2 + x_3 + x_4 + x_5 = 3(a + b + c + d + e)$.
So $540 = 3(a + b + c + d + e) \Rightarrow a + b + c + d + e = 180°$.

$(x_1 + x_2 + x_3 + x_4 + x_5) - (a + b + c + d + e) = 540 - 180 = 360°$.

Method 3:

Draw line l that is parallel to the side AC.

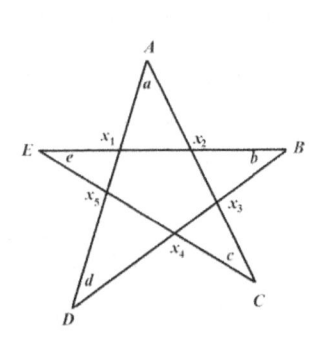

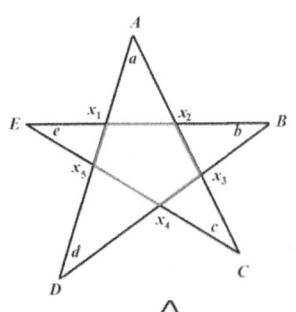

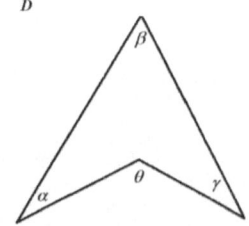

96

So $\angle 1 = \angle 3$, $\angle 2 = \angle 4$.

We also see that $\angle 1 + \angle B + \angle 2 = 180°$ (1)

In triangle CEF, $\angle 3 = \angle 5 + \angle 6$.

In triangle ADG, by $\angle 4 = \angle 7 + \angle 8$.

That is, $\angle 1 = \angle 5 + \angle 6$ (2)

$\angle 2 = \angle 7 + \angle 8$ (3)

Substituting (2) and (3) into (1): $\angle A + \angle B + \angle C + \angle D + \angle D = 180°$.

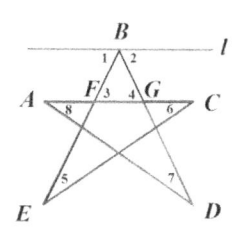

Problem 6. Solution: $1400(\pi - 2)$.

Method 1:

We focus on two circles first. As shown in the figure, AB and O_1O_2 are perpendiculars to each other.

$$AC^2 = O_1A^2 - O_1C^2 \quad \Rightarrow \quad AC = \sqrt{O_1A^2 - O_1C^2} \quad \Rightarrow$$

$$AC = \sqrt{20^2 - 10^2 \times 2} = 10\sqrt{2}.$$

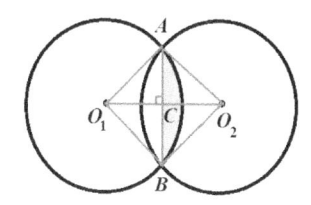

Thus $\angle AO_1B = 90°$. The area of sector AO_1B is

$$\frac{\pi \times AO_1^2}{4} = \frac{\pi \times 20^2}{4} = 100\pi.$$

The shaded area is the same as the difference of the area of sector AO_1B and the area of triangle AO_1B:

$$100\pi - \frac{AB \times O_1C}{2} = 100\pi - \frac{20\sqrt{2} \times 10\sqrt{2}}{2} = 100\pi - 200.$$

The answer will then be $7 \times 2 \times (100\pi - 200) = 1400(\pi - 2)$.

Method 2:

Let x and y be the areas shown in the figure. a is the side length of the square.

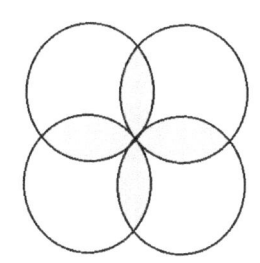

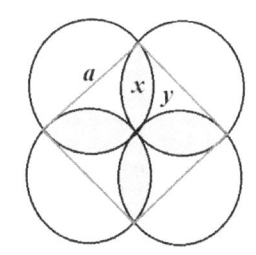

$$\begin{cases} 4x+4y=a^2 \\ 2x+y=\dfrac{\pi(\dfrac{a}{2})^2}{2} \end{cases} \Longrightarrow \begin{cases} 4x+4y=a^2 & (1) \\ 8x+4y=\dfrac{\pi a^2}{8} & (2) \end{cases}$$

$(2)-(1)$: $x=\dfrac{\pi-2}{2}a^2$.

So $4s=\dfrac{\pi-2}{2}a^2=\dfrac{\pi-2}{2}a^2=\dfrac{\pi-2}{2}\times 40^2=800(\pi-2) \Rightarrow s=\dfrac{800(\pi-2)}{4}=200(\pi-2)$.

The answer is $7s=7\times 200(\pi-2)=1400(\pi-2)$.

Problem 7: Solution: 167.

$567 \equiv 138 \pmod{n}$ $\Rightarrow$ $567-138 \equiv 0 \pmod{n}$ $\Rightarrow$ $429 \equiv 0 \pmod{n}$ or $3\times 11 \times 13 \equiv 0 \pmod{n}$ (1)

$366 \equiv 223 \pmod{n}$ $\Rightarrow$ $366-223 \equiv 0 \pmod{n}$ $\Rightarrow$ $143 \equiv 0 \pmod{n}$ or $11 \times 13 \equiv 0 \pmod{n}$ (2)

Comparing (1) and (2) we see that $n=11, 13, 143$.
The sum is $11+13+143=167$.

Problem 8: Solution: 32.

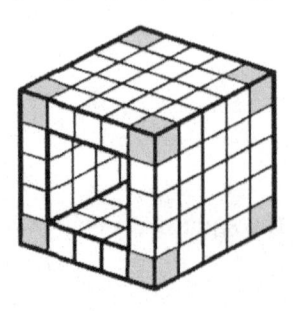

$1\times 8 + 3\times 4 \times 2 = 32$.

Twenty Mathcounts Target Round Tests — Test 12

MATHCOUNTS

■ Mock Competition Twelve ■

Target Round

Name _____

State _____

DO NOT BEGIN UNTIL YOU ARE INSTRUCTED TO DO SO.

This section of the competition consists of eight problems, which will be presented in pairs. Work on one pair of problems will be completed and answers will be collected before the next pair is distributed. The time limit for each pair of problems is six minutes. The first pair of problems is on the other side of this sheet. When told to do so, turn the page over and begin working. Record only final answers in the designated blanks on the problem sheet. All answers must be complete, legible, and simplified to lowest terms. This round assumes the use of calculators, and calculations may also be done on scratch paper, but no other aids are allowed. If you complete the problems before time is called, use the time remaining to check your answers.

Total Correct	Scorer's Initials

Copyright   MYMATHCOUNTS.COM. All rights reserved.

Twenty Mathcounts Target Round Tests   Test 12

1. _____ As shown in the figure, $\angle A = \angle C = 90°$. $AB = AD$. The area of the quadrilateral $ABCD$ is 16. Find the value of $BC + CD$.

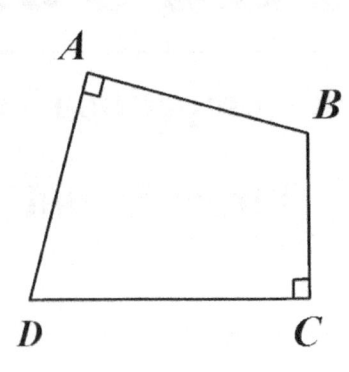

2. _____ As shown in the figure is a 2×3 grid. A, B, C, D, E, F, G, and H are eight points. How many triangles of area 1 are there by using three of these eight points as their vertices?

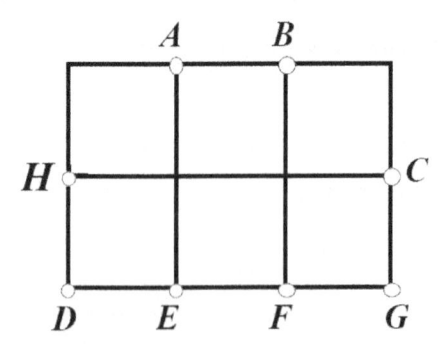

3. _____ The sum of first $5n$ terms in an arithmetic sequence is 2016 more than the sum of its first $2n$ terms. Find the sum of its first $7n$ terms.

4. _____ A, B, and C are three identical pieces of square paper. They are on a square table. The area of A is 64. The visible area of B is 44. The visible area of C is 36. Find the side length of the table.

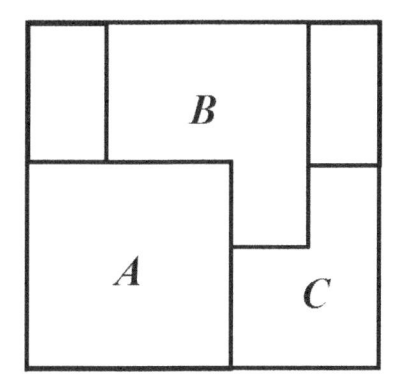

5. _____ $\triangle ABC$ with $\angle A = 90°$. Mark two points D and E on the side of BC such that $BD = BA$, $CE = CA$. If the radius of the inscribed circle to this triangle is 10, find the length of DE.

6. _____ Four distinct positive integers a, b, c, and d have the property that when added in pair, the sums 16, 18, 20, 22, and 24 are obtained. What are the four integers?

7. _____ Two medians of a triangle are perpendicular to each other with one 24 cm long and the other 18 cm. Find the area of the triangle.

8. _____ x and y are positive integers with $x - y = 210$. The least common multiple of x and y is 95 times of their greatest common factor. Find x.

Twenty Mathcounts Target Round Tests — Test 12

SOLUTIONS:

Problem 1: Solution: 8.
Let $\overline{AB} = \overline{AD} = m, \overline{BC} = x, \overline{CD} = y$.

$\overline{BD}^2 = m^2 + m^2 = x^2 + y^2 \quad \Rightarrow \quad x^2 + y^2 = 2m^2$ (1)

$S_{ABCD} = S_{\triangle ABD} + S_{\triangle BCD} = 16 \quad \Rightarrow \quad \dfrac{m^2}{2} + \dfrac{xy}{2} = 16 \quad \Rightarrow \quad m^2 + xy = 32$ (2)

$(2) \times 2 + (1):\ x^2 + 2xy + y^2 = 64 \quad \Rightarrow \quad (x+y)^2 = 64 \quad \Rightarrow \quad x + y = 8 \text{ or } \overline{BC} + \overline{CD} = 8$.

Problem 2: Solution: 16.
$\triangle ABD, \triangle ABE, \triangle ABF, \triangle ABG$.

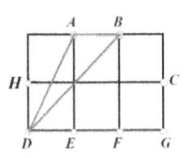

$\triangle CGA, \triangle CGE$

$\triangle HDB, \triangle HDF$

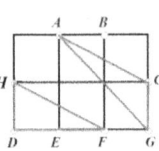

$\triangle DEA, \triangle DEB$.
$\triangle EFA, \triangle EFB$.
$\triangle FGA, \triangle FGB$.

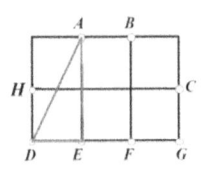

~~$\triangle DFH$,~~ $\triangle DFC$
$\triangle EGH$, ~~$\triangle EGC$~~

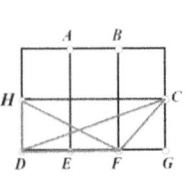

Problem 3: Solution: 4704.
Method 1:
The sums of terms in an arithmetic sequence also form an arithmetic sequence.
Let the 7 sums be $a, a + d, a + 2d, a + 3d, a + 4d, a + 5d, a + 6d$.
$\Rightarrow a + a + d + a + 2d + a + 3d + a + 4d = a + a + d + 2016$
$\Rightarrow 3a + 9d = 2016 \quad \Rightarrow \quad a + 3d = 672$ (which is the middle term).
Thus the sum of the first $7n$ terms $=$ middle term $\times 7 = (a + 3d) \times 7 = 672 \times 7 = 4704$.

Twenty Mathcounts Target Round Tests   **Test 12**

Method 2:

We know that for an arithmetic sequence: $S_{m+n} = (m+n)\dfrac{S_m - S_n}{m-n}$.

$S_{5n+2n} = (5n+2n)\dfrac{S_{5n} - S_{2n}}{5n-2n} = 7n \times \dfrac{2016}{3n} = 4704$.

Problem 4: Solution: 13.

Method 1:

The length of the side of the square A is $\sqrt{64} = 8$. We label the figure as shown.

Then we can write the following equations:

$z(x+y) + (8-z)y = 36 \quad \Rightarrow \quad zx + 8y = 36$ (1)

$8z + (8-z)x = 44 \quad \Rightarrow \quad 8z + 8x - zx = 44$ (2)

$8 + x + y = 8 + z \quad \Rightarrow \quad x + y = z$ (3)

(1) + (2): $8z + 8(x+y) = 80 \quad \Rightarrow \quad z + (x+y) = 10$ (4)

Substituting (3) into (4): $z + z = 10 \quad \Rightarrow \quad z = 5$.

The length of the side of the large square is then $8 + z = 8 + 5 = 13$.

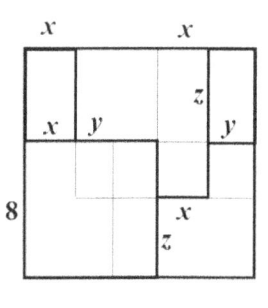

Method 2:

Since $ABCD$ is a square, $AB = 8 + 8 - c = BC = 8 + 8 - a \quad \Rightarrow \quad a = c$.

Now we calculate three shaded areas:

$m = a(b+a) = 20$ (1)

$n = ab$ (2)

$s = (8-a)(8-b)$ (3)

We know that $m + n = 36$. So $ab + (8-a)(8-b) = 36$ (4)

Substituting (1) into (4): $a = 3$.

So the side of the square $ABCD$ is $16 - 3 = 13$.

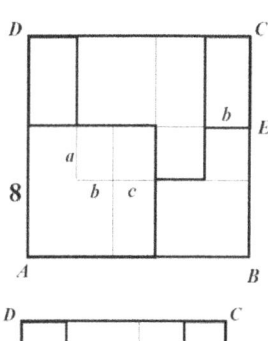

Twenty Mathcounts Target Round Tests   **Test 12**

Problem 5: Solution: 20.

Let $\overline{BD} = \overline{BA} = a, \overline{CE} = \overline{CA} = b, \overline{DE} = x$.

Then $\overline{BC} = a + b - x$.

We know that for the inscribed circle with radius r,

$$r = \frac{\overline{AB} + \overline{AC} - \overline{BC}}{2} \Rightarrow 10 = \frac{\overline{AB} + \overline{AC} - \overline{BC}}{2} \Rightarrow 10 = \frac{a + b - (a + b - x)}{2}$$

$x = 20 = \overline{DE}$.

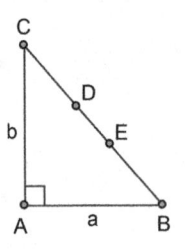

Problem 6: Solution: 7, 9, 11, and 13.

Without loss of generosity, let $a < b < c < d$.

We have: $a + b = 16$ (1)

              $a + c = 18$ (2)

              $b + d = 22$ (3)

              $c + d = 24$ (4)

(1) + (4): $a + b + c + d = 40$ (5)

We know that $a + c = 18$, so $a + d > 18$. We know that $b + d = 22$, so $a + d < 22$.

The only case is that

              $a + d = 20$ (6)

   (3) − (6): $b − a = 2$ (7)

(7) + (1): $b = 9$, and $a = 7$.

Substituting the value of a into (2), and $c = 18 − 7 = 11$.

Substituting the value of b into (3), we get $d = 22 − 9 = 13$.

Four numbers are 7, 9, 11, and 13.

Problem 7: Solution: 288.

$\overline{BE} = 18, \overline{CF} = 24.$ $\overline{GE} = 18 \times \frac{1}{3} = 6, \overline{CG} = 24 \times \frac{2}{3} = 16.$ $S_{\triangle CGE} = \frac{16 \times 6}{2} = 48$.

Since 6 smaller triangles have the same area,

$S_{\triangle ABC} = 6 \times S_{\triangle CGE} = 6 \times 48 = 288$.

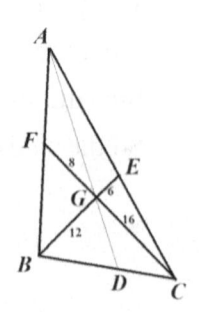

106

Problem 8: Solution: 285.

Let $x = dh$ and $y = dk$. h and k are relatively prime.

We know that $x > y$. So $h > k$.

Thus $dhk = 95d \quad \Rightarrow \quad hk = 95$.

Since h and k are relatively prime, $h = 95, k = 1$; or $h = 19, k = 5$.

We also know that $dh - dk = 210 \quad \Rightarrow \quad d(h - k) = 210$.

Thus $h - k$ is a factor of 210.

Therefore $h = 19$ and $k = 5$.

When $h - k = 14$, $d = 15$.

$x = 15 \times 19 = 285$.

MATHCOUNTS

■ Mock Competition Thirteen ■

Target Round

Name _____

State _____

DO NOT BEGIN UNTIL YOU ARE INSTRUCTED TO DO SO.

This section of the competition consists of eight problems, which will be presented in pairs. Work on one pair of problems will be completed and answers will be collected before the next pair is distributed. The time limit for each pair of problems is six minutes. The first pair of problems is on the other side of this sheet. When told to do so, turn the page over and begin working. Record only final answers in the designated blanks on the problem sheet. All answers must be complete, legible, and simplified to lowest terms. This round assumes the use of calculators, and calculations may also be done on scratch paper, but no other aids are allowed. If you complete the problems before time is called, use the time remaining to check your answers.

Total Correct	Scorer's Initials

Copyright   MYMATHCOUNTS.COM. All rights reserved.

Twenty Mathcounts Target Round Tests Test 13

1. _____ Given that ∠ADB = ∠CBA, AD = 3 and CD = 7, how many units are in the length of $\overline{AB}$? Express your answer as a decimal rounded to the nearest tenth.

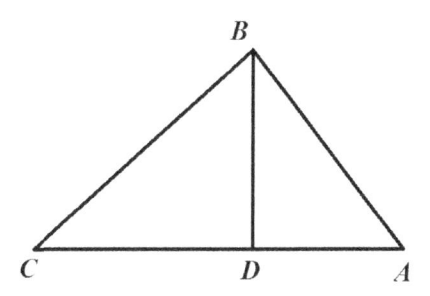

2. _____ The number 2015 can be written as the sum of consecutive positive integers in several ways. When written as the sum of the greatest possible number of consecutive positive integers, what is the largest of these integers?

Twenty Mathcounts Target Round Tests   **Test 13**

3. _____ Pentagon *ABCDE* is formed by connecting *A* and *E*, the midpoints of two consecutive sides of a square. What is the sum of the lengths of the diagonals of the pentagon, expressed as a decimal rounded to the nearest tenth?

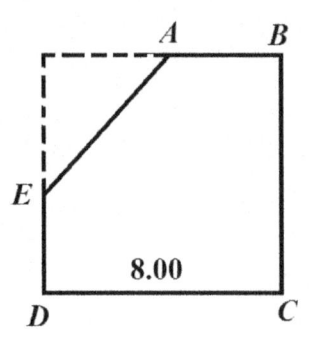

4. _____ What is the few number of L-shaped trominoes, as shown below, that can be entirely placed on the 6 × 6 grid shown so that no more tromino can be placed on the board without overlapping? The small squares are all congruent.

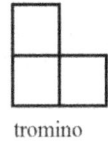

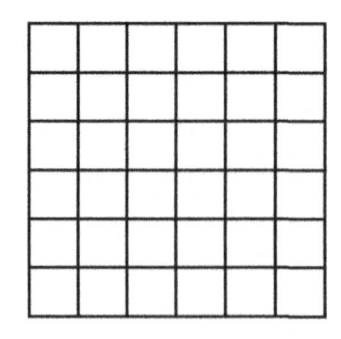

tromino

5. _____ What is the value of $\dfrac{3}{2}+\dfrac{5}{2}+\dfrac{7}{2}+\cdots+\dfrac{2013}{2}$?

6. _____ How many ordered pairs of distinct positive integers (m, n) are there so that the sum of the reciprocals of m and n is $\dfrac{1}{6}$?

Twenty Mathcounts Target Round Tests   **Test 13**

7. _____ Compute the sum of a, b and c given that $\dfrac{a}{3} = \dfrac{b}{4} = \dfrac{c}{5}$ and $abc = 1620$.

8. _____ This figure has a total area of 216 square units and is a rectangle composed of three congruent, smaller rectangles. Find the sum of the length and width of one of the smaller rectangles.

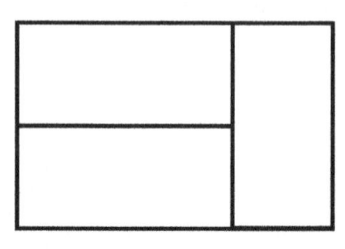

Twenty Mathcounts Target Round Tests   Test 13

SOLUTIONS:

Problem 1: Solution: 5.5.

We see that triangle ABC is similar to triangle ADB. So the corresponding sides are proportional: $\dfrac{AC}{AB} = \dfrac{AB}{AD} \Rightarrow AB^2 = AC \times AD = 10 \times 3$

$\Rightarrow AB = \sqrt{10 \times 3} \approx 5.5$.

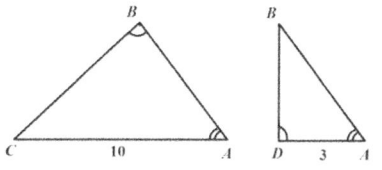

Problem 2: Solution: 63.

For some positive integers m and k,

$$N = m + (m+1) + (m+2) + (m+3) + \ldots + (m+k-1) = \dfrac{(m+m+k-1)k}{2} = \dfrac{(2m+k-1)k}{2}$$

So $2N = (2m + k - 1)k$.

We are looking for the greatest possible value of k. We know that $k < 2m + k - 1$ and that k and $2m + k - 1$ have different parity, so we set the value for k so that it is as close as possible to $2m + k - 1$: $k(2m + k - 1) = 2 \times 2015 = 2 \times 5 \times 13 \times 31 = 62 \times 65$.

So $k = 62$ and $2m + k - 1 = 65$. We get $m = 2$.

The value of the greatest term $= m + k - 1 = 2 + 62 - 1 = 63$.

Indeed, $2 + 3 + 4 + \ldots + 63 = 2015$.

Problem 3: Solution: 47.1.

We have 5 diagonals: DA, AC, CE, EB, BD. Among them,

$DA = AC = CE = EB = \sqrt{8^2 + 4^2} = 4\sqrt{5}$.

$BD = \sqrt{8^2 + 8^2} = 8\sqrt{2}$.

The sum is $4 \times 4\sqrt{5} + 8\sqrt{2} \approx 47.1$

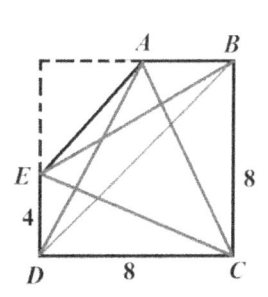

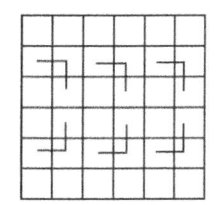

Problem 4: Solution: 6.

113

Twenty Mathcounts Target Round Tests   Test 13

Problem 5: Solution: 507024.

We have $2013 = 3 + (n-1)2 \Rightarrow n = 1006$ terms.

The sum will be $\dfrac{3}{2} + \dfrac{5}{2} + \dfrac{7}{2} + \cdots + \dfrac{2013}{2} = \dfrac{(3+2013)1006}{2 \times 2} = 507024$.

Or the sum will be $(1007^2 - 1)/2 = 507024$.

Problem 6. Solution: 8.

The given equation can be written as: $6y + 6x = xy$, or

$xy - 6x - 6x = 0 \Rightarrow (x-6)(y-6) = 36$

The following equations will have of solutions:

$(x-6)(y-6) = 1 \times 36$ (2 pairs)
$(x-6)(y-6) = 2 \times 18$ (2 pairs)
$(x-6)(y-6) = 3 \times 12$ (2 pairs)
$(x-6)(y-6) = 4 \times 9$ (2 pairs)
$(x-6)(y-6) = 6 \times 6$ (1 pair)

Since x and y are distinct, we have $9 - 1 = 8$ pairs.

Problem 7: Solution: 36.

Let $\dfrac{a}{3} = \dfrac{b}{4} = \dfrac{c}{5} = \dfrac{a+b+c}{12} = k$. So $a = 3k$, $b = 4k$, $c = 5k$.

$abc = 1620 \Rightarrow (3k)(4k)(5k) = 1620 \Rightarrow k^3 = 27 \Rightarrow k = 3$

$\dfrac{a+b+c}{12} = k \Rightarrow a+b+c = 12k = 12 \times 3 = 36$.

Problem 8: Solution: 18.

We label the figure as follows:

We have $(x+y) \times (2y) = 216$ (1)
               $x = 2y$ (2)

Substituting (2) into (1):

$(2y+y) \times (2y) = 216 \Rightarrow 6y^2 = 216 \Rightarrow y^2 = 36 \Rightarrow$

$y = 6$.

$x = 2y = 12$. $x + y = 12 + 6 = 18$.

Twenty Mathcounts Target Round Tests Test 14

MATHCOUNTS

■ Mock Competition Fourteen ■

Target Round

Name _____

State _____

DO NOT BEGIN UNTIL YOU ARE INSTRUCTED TO DO SO.

This section of the competition consists of eight problems, which will be presented in pairs. Work on one pair of problems will be completed and answers will be collected before the next pair is distributed. The time limit for each pair of problems is six minutes. The first pair of problems is on the other side of this sheet. When told to do so, turn the page over and begin working. Record only final answers in the designated blanks on the problem sheet. All answers must be complete, legible, and simplified to lowest terms. This round assumes the use of calculators, and calculations may also be done on scratch paper, but no other aids are allowed. If you complete the problems before time is called, use the time remaining to check your answers.

Total Correct	Scorer's Initials

Copyright   MYMATHCOUNTS.COM. All rights reserved.

Twenty Mathcounts Target Round Tests Test 14

1. _____ All the students in Alex's class are standing in a row. Mrs. Leighton counts them from left to right this way: 1, 2, 3; 1, 2, 3; 1, 2, 3; and so on. The last student is counted as "2". Mr. Leighton then counts them from right to left this way: 1, 2, 3, 4; 1, 2, 3, 4; 1, 2, 3, 4; and so on. The last student is counted as "3". If 5 students are counted as "1" in both counts, how many students are in Alex's class?

2. _____ As shown in the figure, $\angle BAC = 90°$. E is the midpoint of AB. $\angle AEC = \angle BAD$. $DC = 10$. Find BC.

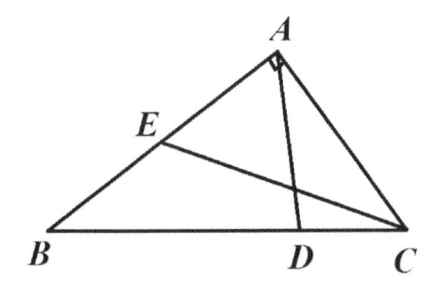

Twenty Mathcounts Target Round Tests   **Test 14**

3. _____ For a three-digit number $\overline{abc}$, if $0 < a < b < c$, then this number is called a "good number". Arrange all the "good numbers" in a row in the order of smallest to greatest. What is the 45th "good number"?

4. _____ There are eight positive numbers arranged in a row from left to right. Starting from the third term, every term is the product of the two numbers before it. The 5th term is 3, and the 8th term is 243. Find the first term.

5. _____ The number of consecutive positive integers is even and the sum of them is 2014. Find the greatest one among these consecutive positive integers.

6. _____ A box contains balls of three colors: red, yellow, and white. The number of white balls is at most 1/2 of the number of yellow balls, and at least 1/3 of red balls. The sum of the number of yellow balls and the number of white balls is less than or equal to 54. At most how many red balls are in the box?

7. _____ Natural numbers 1 to 6 are used to label six faces of a cube with one number on each face. Alex has five such identical cubes and he arranges them in a row as shown in the figure. What is the number that is on the face opposite to the face with a "4" on it?

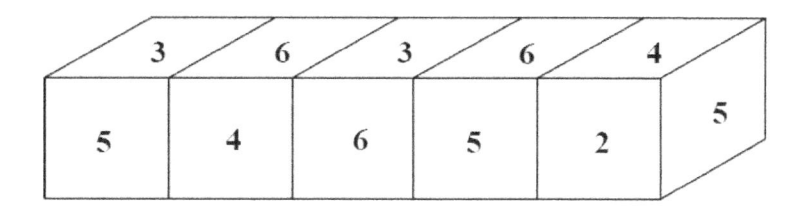

8. _____ A series is as follows: 0, 1, 0, 1, 1, 0, 1, 1, 1, 0, 1, 1, 1, 1, 0, ...The pattern is that there is one "1" between two zeros first, then there are two "1" between two zeros, and each time a "1" is added between two zeros. Find the sum of the first 2014 terms in the series.

Twenty Mathcounts Target Round Tests   Test 14

SOLUTIONS:

Problem 1: Solution: 59.

Method 1:
123123│1│23123123……123│1│2312
321432│1│43214321……432│1│4321

So the seventh person is counted as "1". We also know that the least common multiple of 3 and 4 is 12. Thus the next person who counts "1" will be the 7 + 12 = 19th person in the line. The number of students in Alex's class is 7 + (5 − 1) × 12 + 4 = 59.

Method 2:
Let the number of students in the class is n.

$$\begin{cases} n \equiv 2 \mod 3 \\ n \equiv 3 \mod 4 \end{cases} \Longrightarrow \begin{cases} n \equiv 2 \mod 3 \\ n \equiv 3 \mod 4 \end{cases} \Longrightarrow n \equiv 11 \mod 12$$

So n can be 11, 23, 35, 47, 59, 71,…

Since 5 students are counted as "1" in both counts, we know the number is the 5th number (59) on the list above.

Problem 2: Solution: 30.

Method 1:
$\angle BAC = 90° \Rightarrow \angle 1 + \angle 3 = \angle 2 + \angle 4 = 90°$.
$\angle 1 = \angle 2 \quad \Rightarrow \quad \angle 3 = \angle 4 \quad \Rightarrow \quad \overline{EG} = \overline{AG} = \overline{GC}$.
Draw $\overline{EF} \parallel \overline{AD}$ to meet $\overline{BC}$ at F.
$\overline{FD} = \overline{DC} = 10$

Since E is the midpoint of $\overline{AB}, \overline{BF} = \overline{FD} = 10$.

Thus $\overline{BC} = 10 + 10 + 10 = 30$.

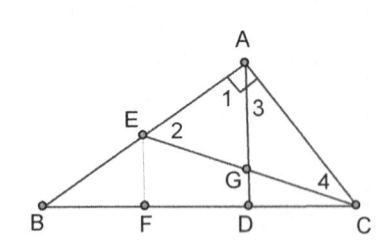

Method 2:
We know that $\overline{EG} = \overline{AG}$ and $\angle BAC = 90°$. So AG is the median of right triangle AEC and $AG = EG = GC$.

We draw $EF//BC$ to meet AD at F. $\triangle GEF$ is congruent to $\triangle GCD$. Thus $EF = CD = 10$.

We also know that $EF = \frac{1}{2}BD \Rightarrow BD = 2EF = 2 \times 10 = 20$.

$BC = BD + DC = 20 + 10 = 30$.

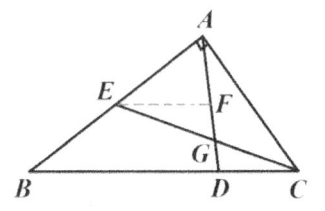

Problem 3: Solution: 268.

For the case the left most digit is 1:

If tens digit is 2, hundred digit can be 3 to 9. There are 7 such numbers.

If tens digit is 3, hundred digit can be 4 to 9. There are 6 such numbers.

And so on. We have $7 + 6 + 5 + 4 + 3 + 2 + 1 = 28$ such numbers.

For the case the left most digit is 2, we have $6 + 5 + 4 + 3 + 2 + 1 = 21$ such numbers.

So we have $28 + 21 = 49$ such numbers. The 49th number is the last number starting with the digit 2. So it is 289. We count backward: 279, 278, 269. The 45th number is 268.

Problem 4: Solution: $\frac{1}{3}$.

Let the terms be $a, b, ab, ab^2, a^2b^3, a^3b^5, a^5b^8, a^8b^{13}$.

$\begin{cases} a^2b^3 = 3 & (1) \\ a^8b^{13} = 243 & (2) \end{cases}$

$(1)^4 : a^4b^{12} = 2^4 = 16$ (3)

$(2) \div (3): b = 3$

Substituting $b = 3$ into (1): $a^2 \times 27 = 3 \Rightarrow a = \frac{1}{3}$.

Problem 5: Solution: 505.

Let these consecutive positive integers be $m, m+1, m+2, \cdots, m+(k-1)$.

$S = \frac{k(2m+k-1)}{2} = 2014$.

k and $2m + k - 1$ have the opposite parity and $k < 2m + k - 1$.

So $k(2m+k-1) = 4028 = 2 \times 2 \times 19 \times 53$

Since we want the greatest value for the last term of these consecutive integers, we set $k = 4$ (as small as possible) and then $2m + k - 1 = 2m + 4 - 1 = 19 \times 53 \Rightarrow m = 502$. The last term is $502 + 3 = 505$.

Twenty Mathcounts Target Round Tests — **Test 14**

Problem 6: Solution: 54.

Let w, y and r be the numbers of white, yellow, and red balls, respectively.

$$w \le \frac{1}{2}y \tag{1}$$

$$w \ge \frac{1}{3}r \quad \Rightarrow \quad \frac{1}{3}r \le w \tag{2}$$

$$y + w \le 54 \tag{3}$$

$$(1) + (2): \quad \frac{1}{3}r \le \frac{1}{2}y \quad \Rightarrow \quad 2r \le 3y \tag{4}$$

$$3 \times (3): \quad 3y + 3w \le 3 \times 54 \tag{5}$$

$$(4) + (5): \quad 2r \le 3 \times 54 - 3w \tag{6}$$

Substituting (2) into (6):

$$2r \le 3 \times 54 - 3 \times \frac{1}{3}r \quad \Rightarrow \quad 3r \le 3 \times 54 \quad \Rightarrow \quad r \le 54.$$

The greatest value for r is 54. We checked and 54 works.

Problem 7: Solution: 3.

5 is next to 3, 6, 2, and 4. So 5 is facing 1.

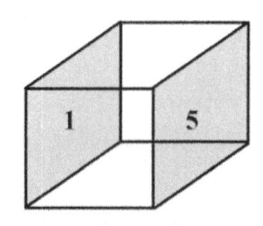

4 is next to 2, 5, 6.

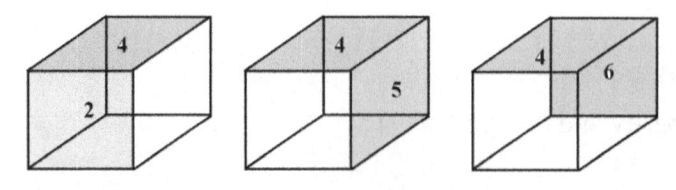

We already know that 1 is facing 5. So only 3 is available to face 4.

Twenty Mathcounts Target Round Tests   **Test 14**

Problem 8: Solution: 1952.

We group the series this way:

0 | 10 | 110 | 1110 | 11110 | …

The numbers of terms in each group are 1, 2, 3,….We see that in nth group, there are $n-1$ 1's and one 0.

Let the sequence be b_n and $b_n = 1 + 2 + 3 + \cdots + n = \dfrac{n(n+1)}{2}$.

We know that $b_n \le 2014$ $\Rightarrow$ $\dfrac{n(n+1)}{2} \le 2014$ $\Rightarrow$ $n(n+1) \le 4028$.

We see that $\dfrac{62(62+1)}{2} = 1953 \le 2014 \le \dfrac{63(63+1)}{2} = 2016$. Thus $n = 62$.

When $n = 62$, $b_n = 1953$. We need to have more terms in order to get 2014 terms. In the group $n = 63$, the first 62 numbers are 1 and the last number is 0. Since $1953 + 62 = 2015 > 2014$, the last 0 does not count. Therefore, the first 2014 terms contain 62 zeros. The sum of the first 2014 terms is $2014 - 62 = 1952$.

MATCHCOUNTS

■ Mock Competition Fifteen ■

Target Round

Name _____

State _____

DO NOT BEGIN UNTIL YOU ARE INSTRUCTED TO DO SO.

This section of the competition consists of eight problems, which will be presented in pairs. Work on one pair of problems will be completed and answers will be collected before the next pair is distributed. The time limit for each pair of problems is six minutes. The first pair of problems is on the other side of this sheet. When told to do so, turn the page over and begin working. Record only final answers in the designated blanks on the problem sheet. All answers must be complete, legible, and simplified to lowest terms. This round assumes the use of calculators, and calculations may also be done on scratch paper, but no other aids are allowed. If you complete the problems before time is called, use the time remaining to check your answers.

Total Correct	Scorer's Initials

Copyright   MYMATHCOUNTS.COM. All rights reserved.

Twenty Mathcounts Target Round Tests   **Test 15**

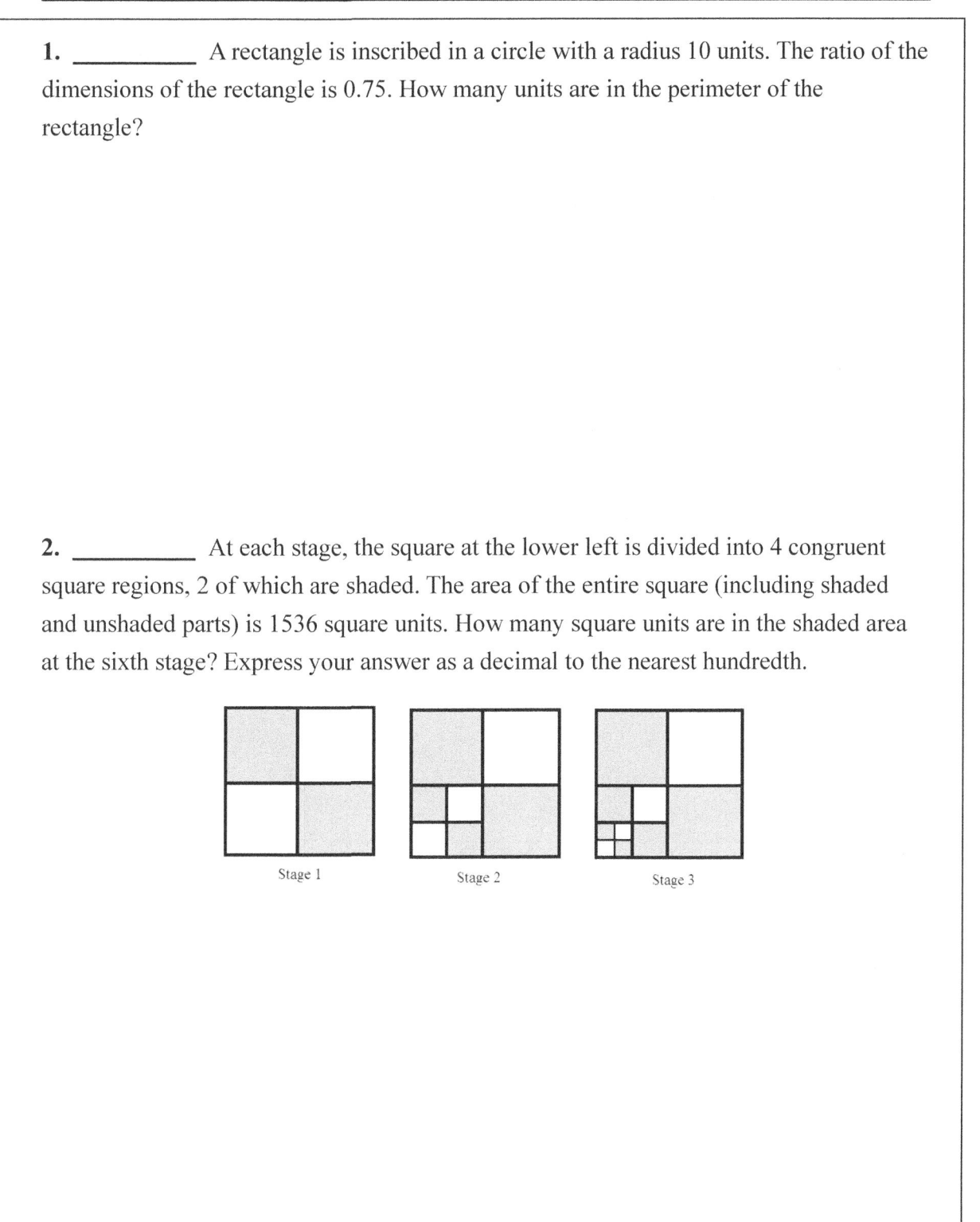

1. _____ A rectangle is inscribed in a circle with a radius 10 units. The ratio of the dimensions of the rectangle is 0.75. How many units are in the perimeter of the rectangle?

2. _____ At each stage, the square at the lower left is divided into 4 congruent square regions, 2 of which are shaded. The area of the entire square (including shaded and unshaded parts) is 1536 square units. How many square units are in the shaded area at the sixth stage? Express your answer as a decimal to the nearest hundredth.

Stage 1   Stage 2   Stage 3

Twenty Mathcounts Target Round Tests　　　　　　　　　　**Test 15**

3. _____ A data set consists of the 171 digits used to write all the natural numbers from 1 to 90 inclusive. What is the arithmetic mean of the digits in the data set? Express your answer as a decimal rounded to the nearest tenth.

4. _____ Randomly select a whole number x such that $0 < x < 101$. What is the probability that x equals the sum of two perfect squares? Note that zero is a square number. Express your answer as a fraction.

Twenty Mathcounts Target Round Tests   **Test 15**

5. _____ Unit cubes are glued together to make a cube several units on each side. Some of the faces of this large cube are painted. When the cube is taken apart, there are exactly 49 unit cubes without any paint. How many unit cubes were used to create the larger cube?

6. _____ How many positive three-digit numbers are there such that the sum of the three digits is 11?

Twenty Mathcounts Target Round Tests Test 15

7. _____ The sum of the reciprocals of the three consecutive positive integers is greater than 1. What is the least number of consecutive positive integers necessary to make the sum of the reciprocals greater than two?

8. _____ Two circles are internally tangent. The smaller circle is also tangent to two perpendicular radii of the larger circle. What is the ratio of the circumference of the small circle to the circumference of the large circle? Express your answer as a simplest radical form.

Problem 1: Solution: 56.

Since $\angle B = 90°$, the diameter of the circle is the diagonal of the rectangle $ABCD$.
We know that the ratio of the dimensions of the rectangle is $0.75 = 3/4$.
So let one dimension be $3x$ and the other dimension be $4x$.
Applying Pythagorean Theorem to triangle ABC:
$(3x)^2 + (4x)^2 = 20^2$ $\Rightarrow$ $x^2 = 16$ $\Rightarrow$ $x = 4$.
So the perimeter of the rectangle is $2(3 \times 4 + 4 \times 4) = 56$.

Problem 2: Solution: 1023.75.

The fractions of the shaded areas for stages 1 through 6 are

$\dfrac{2}{4}$, $\dfrac{2}{4}+\dfrac{2}{4^2}$, $\dfrac{2}{4}+\dfrac{2}{4^2}+\dfrac{2}{4^3}$, $\dfrac{2}{4}+\dfrac{2}{4^2}+\dfrac{2}{4^3}+\dfrac{2}{4^4}$, $\dfrac{2}{4}+\dfrac{2}{4^2}+\dfrac{2}{4^3}+\dfrac{2}{4^4}+\dfrac{2}{4^5}$,

$\dfrac{2}{4}+\dfrac{2}{4^2}+\dfrac{2}{4^3}+\dfrac{2}{4^4}+\dfrac{2}{4^5}+\dfrac{2}{4^6}$.

The shaded area for the sixth stage is $1536 \times (\dfrac{2}{4}+\dfrac{2}{4^2}+\dfrac{2}{4^3}+\dfrac{2}{4^4}+\dfrac{2}{4^5}+\dfrac{2}{4^6}) = 1023.75$.

Problem 3: Solution: 4.5.

Pages 1 – 9: $1 + 2 + 3 +…+ 9 = 45$.
Pages 10 – 19: $10 \times 1 + 45$.
Pages 20 – 29: $10 \times 2 + 45$.
……
Pages 80 – 89: $10 \times 8 + 45$.
Page 90: 9.
The sum is $45 + 10 \times 1 + 45 + 10 \times 2 + 45 + …+ 10 \times 8 + 45 + 9 = 10(1 + 2 + …+ 8) + 9 \times 45 + 9 = 774$.
The arithmetic mean of the digits is $774/171 \approx 4.5$.

Problem 4: Solution: 23/50.

We look at all the numbers from 1 to 100 inclusive for x.
We have the following list:

Twenty Mathcounts Target Round Tests   **Test 15**

$1^2 + 1^2, 1^2 + 2^2, \ldots, 1^2 + 9^2$. We have 9 such numbers.

$2^2 + 2^2, 2^2 + 3^2, \ldots, 2^2 + 9^2$. We have 8 such numbers.

$3^2 + 3^2, 3^2 + 4^2, \ldots, 3^2 + 9^2$. We have 7 such numbers.

$4^2 + 4^2, 4^2 + 5^2, \ldots, 4^2 + 9^2$. We have 6 such numbers.

$5^2 + 5^2, 5^2 + 6^2, \ldots, 5^2 + 8^2$. We have 4 such numbers.

$6^2 + 6^2, 6^2 + 7^2, 6^2 + 8^2$. We have 3 such numbers.

$7^2 + 7^2$. We have 1 such number.

So far we have $9 + 8 + 7 + 6 + 4 + 3 + 1 = 38$ such x's.

Now we look at all square numbers. We have 10 square numbers from $1^2 = 1^2 + 0^2$ to 10^2. However, we already count $5^2 = 3^2 + 4^2$ and $10^2 = 6^2 + 8^2$.

So the total number is $38 + 8 = 46$. The probability is $46/100 = 23/50$.

Problem 5: Solution: 125.

For the larger cube of $n \times n \times n$, the number of cubes with zero side painted is $(n-2)^3$. 49 is not a cubic number. The possible numbers of cubes with zero side painted are 8, or 27. Since there are 49 cubes painted zero side, n can only be 5. The number of unit cubes used to create the larger cube is then $5^3 = 125$.

Problem 6.   Solution: 61.

Method 1:

We do an organized list:

9   2   0   (4 rearrangements: 920, 902, 290, 209)

9   1   1   (3 rearrangements: 3!/2!)

8   3   0   (4 rearrangements)

8   2   1   (6 rearrangements: 3!)

7   4   0   (4 rearrangements)

7   3   1   (6 rearrangements)

7   2   2   (3 rearrangements)

6   5   0   (4 rearrangements)

6   4   1   (6 rearrangements)

6   3   2   (6 rearrangements)

5   5   1   (3 rearrangements)

Twenty Mathcounts Target Round Tests **Test 15**

5 4 2   (6 rearrangements)
5 3 3   (3 rearrangements)
4 4 3   (3 rearrangements)
Total $4 + 3 + 4 + 6 + 4 + 6 + 3 + 4 + 6 + 6 + 3 + 6 + 3 + 3 = 61$.

Method 2:

To find the number of solutions to $x_1 + x_2 + x_3 = 11$ with restrictions $1 \leq x_1 \leq 9$, $0 \leq x_2 \leq 9$, and $0 \leq x_3 \leq 9$, we first calculate the number of positive integer solutions:

$$N_1 = \binom{11-1}{2} = \binom{10}{2} = 45.$$

We still need to, however, calculate N_2, the number of 3-digit numbers containing zero in the ten's or one's digits. This can easily be done by listing. We know that ten's and one's digit can't both be zero since they must add up to 11. The 3-digit numbers containing zero in the units digit can be listed below:

9 2 0   (4 rearrangements: 920, 902, 290, 209)
8 3 0   (4 rearrangements)
7 4 0   (4 rearrangements)
6 5 0   (4 rearrangements)
So $N_2 = 16$.
$N = N_1 + N_2 = 45 + 16 = 61$.

Method 3:

The number of solutions to the equation: $x_1 + x_2 + x_3 = 11$ (with the restrictions $1 \leq x_1 \leq 9$, and $0 \leq x_i \leq 9$, $i = 2, 3$): $N = N_1 - N_2$

N_1, the number of non-negative integer solutions of the above equation:

$$N_1 = \binom{11+3-1}{3-1} - \binom{3}{1}\binom{11+3-1\times 10 -1}{3-1} = 78 - 9 = 69$$

N_2, the number of non-negative integer solutions to the equation: $y_1 + y_2 = 11$ (with the restrictions $0 \le y_i \le 9$, $i = 1, 2$):

$$N_2 = \binom{11+2-1}{2-1} - \binom{2}{1}\binom{11+2-1 \times 10 - 1}{2-1} = 12 - 4 = 8$$

The desired solution is then $N_1 - N_2 = 69 - 8 = 61$.

Problem 7: Solution: 11.

Method 1:

The fastest way is to use the calculator and keep adding the consecutive fractions until

$$\frac{1}{2} + \frac{1}{3} + \frac{1}{4} + \ldots + \frac{1}{n} > 2$$

$n = 11$.

Method 2:

First we try $n = 10$

Since $\frac{1}{2} + \frac{1}{3} + \frac{1}{6} = 1$, we only need to check if $\frac{1}{4} + \frac{1}{5} + \frac{1}{7} + \frac{1}{8} + \frac{1}{9} + \frac{1}{10} > 1$.

$$\frac{1}{4} + \frac{1}{5} + \frac{1}{7} + \frac{1}{8} + \frac{1}{9} + \frac{1}{10} = (\frac{1}{4} + \frac{1}{8}) + (\frac{1}{5} + \frac{1}{10}) + \frac{1}{7} + \frac{1}{9}$$

$$= \frac{3}{8} + \frac{3}{10} + \frac{1}{7} + \frac{1}{9} < \frac{3}{8} + \frac{3}{10} + \frac{1}{5} + \frac{1}{8} = \frac{1}{2} + \frac{1}{2} = 1$$

So n should be more than 10. We add one more term $\frac{1}{11}$ in our calculation:

$$\frac{3}{8} + \frac{3}{10} + \frac{1}{7} + \frac{1}{9} + \frac{1}{11} = 3(\frac{1}{8} + \frac{1}{10}) + \frac{1}{7} + (\frac{1}{9} + \frac{1}{11})$$

$$> 3 \times \frac{4}{18} + \frac{1}{7} + \frac{4}{20} = \frac{2}{3} + \frac{1}{7} + \frac{1}{5} > \frac{2}{3} + \frac{4}{12} = 1$$

So we know that $n = 11$.

Problem 8: Solution: $\sqrt{2}-1$.

Let R be the radius of the large circle and r be the radius of the large circle.
Applying Pythagorean Theorem, we get: $r^2 + r^2 = (R-r)^2 \Rightarrow 2r^2 = (R-r)^2$
We know that $R > r$. So we have $\sqrt{2}r = R - r \Rightarrow$

$$\sqrt{2}r + r = R \Rightarrow (\sqrt{2}+1)r = R$$

$$\Rightarrow \frac{r}{R} = \frac{1}{\sqrt{2}+1} = \sqrt{2}-1.$$

We know that the ratio of the circumferences is
$\dfrac{2\pi r}{2\pi R} = \dfrac{r}{R} = \sqrt{2}-1$.

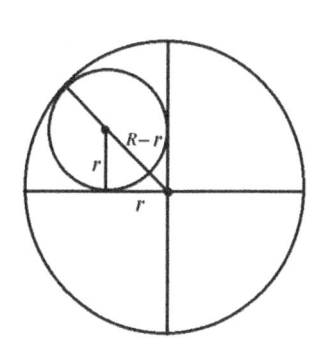

Twenty Mathcounts Target Round Tests   **Test 16**

MATHCOUNTS

■ **Mock Competition Sixteen** ■

Target Round

Name _____

State _____

DO NOT BEGIN UNTIL YOU ARE INSTRUCTED TO DO SO.

This section of the competition consists of eight problems, which will be presented in pairs. Work on one pair of problems will be completed and answers will be collected before the next pair is distributed. The time limit for each pair of problems is six minutes. The first pair of problems is on the other side of this sheet. When told to do so, turn the page over and begin working. Record only final answers in the designated blanks on the problem sheet. All answers must be complete, legible, and simplified to lowest terms. This round assumes the use of calculators, and calculations may also be done on scratch paper, but no other aids are allowed. If you complete the problems before time is called, use the time remaining to check your answers.

Total Correct	Scorer's Initials

Copyright   MYMATHCOUNTS.COM. All rights reserved.

Twenty Mathcounts Target Round Tests — Test 16

1. _____ Quadrilateral $ABCD$ with $\angle BAD = 120°$, $\angle BCD = 60°$, $\angle ABC = \angle ADC = 90°$. $AB = 8\sqrt{3}$, $BC = 36$. Find CD.

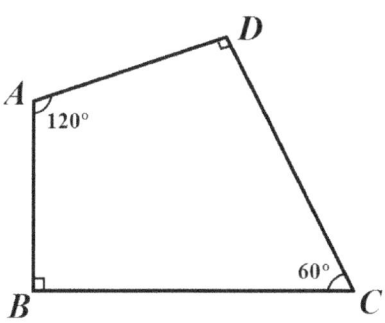

2. _____ Container A has three balls, labeled 1, 2, and 3 as shown in the figure. Containers B and C are empty and identical to A in shape. Your task is to move three balls from A to C via B. You are allowed only to move balls from left to right and move one ball at a time. How many ways are there to move all three balls to C?

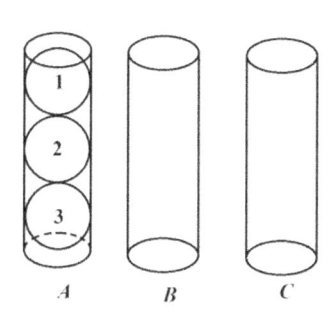

3. _____ If $f(x) = x + \sqrt{3-x}$, x is real number and $x \leq 3$, what is the greatest value of $f(x)$?

4. _____ Find the sum of the digits of the quotient when the 66-digit number $\underbrace{66666...6666}_{66 \ 6\text{'s}}$ is divided by 7.

Twenty Mathcounts Target Round Tests Test 16

5. _____ There are 20 5-gram weights and 20 3-gram weighs. How many different ways are there to weigh a ball that is 1 gram? Note that 5-gram weights can only be put into the left pan of the scale and 3-gram weights can only be put into the right pan of the scale.

6. _____ G is on the side BC of the square $ABCD$ with $AB = 12$. The side EF of the rectangle $DEFG$ passes through A. $GD = 13$. Find FG.

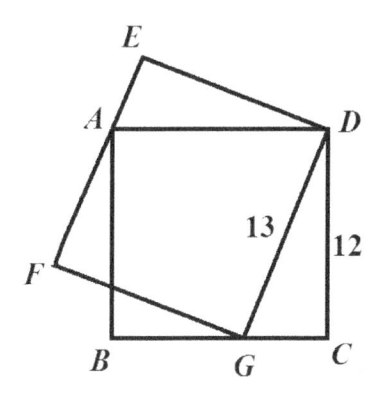

7. _____ Positive integers are arranged as follows. The number 2014 is in *n*th row and *m*th column counting from left to right from the first number in this row. What is *n* + *m*?

Row								
1				1				
2			2	3	4			
3		5	6	7	8	9		
4	10	11	12	13	14	15	16	
…	…	…	…	…	…	…	…	

8. _____ Each face of a cube is written a positive integer selected from 2 to 15. Each vertex of the cube is also written a positive integer such that the positive integer in the vertex is the product of the three numbers on the faces that share the vertex. The sum of the positive integers of all vertices is 585. Find the sum of the six positive integers on the faces of the cube.

Twenty Mathcounts Target Round Tests   Test 16

SOLUTIONS:

Problem 1: Solution: 30.

Method 1:

Draw $AE \parallel BC$ and to meet DC at E. Draw $EF \perp BC$ at F.
$ABFE$ is a rectangle with $EF = AB = 8\sqrt{3}$.
$\angle C = 60° \Rightarrow FC = 8, EC = 16$. So $BF = 36 - 8 = 28 = AE$.

Since $\angle DAE = 120° - 90° = 30°$, $DE = \dfrac{1}{2} AE = 14$. Thus $CD = DE + EC = 14 + 16 = 30$.

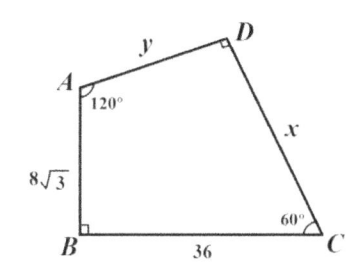

Method 2:

Let DC be x and AD be y as shown in the figure.
We calculate the area by two different ways:

$$\frac{1}{2} y \times 8\sqrt{3} \sin 120° + \frac{1}{2} x \times 36 \sin 60° = \frac{1}{2} 36 \times 8\sqrt{3} + \frac{1}{2} xy \qquad (1)$$

By Pythagorean Theorem, we have $x^2 + y^2 = 36^2 + (8\sqrt{3})^2$ (2)

Solving the system of equations by a calculator, we get the only solution:

$x = 30$ and $y = 14\sqrt{3}$.

Problem 2: Solution: 5 ways.

$1 \Rightarrow B \Rightarrow C;\quad 2 \Rightarrow B \Rightarrow C;\quad 3 \Rightarrow B \Rightarrow C.$
$1 \Rightarrow B \Rightarrow C;\quad 2 \Rightarrow B;\quad 3 \Rightarrow B \Rightarrow C;\quad 2 \Rightarrow C.$
$1 \Rightarrow B;\quad 2 \Rightarrow B \Rightarrow C;\quad 1 \Rightarrow C;\quad 3 \Rightarrow C.$
$1 \Rightarrow B;\quad 2 \Rightarrow B \Rightarrow C;\quad 3 \Rightarrow B \Rightarrow C;\quad 1 \Rightarrow C.$
$1 \Rightarrow B;\quad 2 \Rightarrow B;\quad 3 \Rightarrow B \Rightarrow C;\quad 2 \Rightarrow C; 1 \Rightarrow C.$

Note: the general formula for n balls is $\binom{2n}{n} - \binom{2n}{n-1}$.

Problem 3: Solution: $\dfrac{13}{4}$.

Twenty Mathcounts Target Round Tests   **Test 16**

Method 1:

Let $3 - x = t^2 \Rightarrow x = 3 - t^2$

$y = 3 - t^2 + t = -t^2 + t + 3 = -(t - \frac{1}{2})^2 + \frac{13}{4}$.

When $t = \frac{1}{2}$, y has the greatest value of $\frac{13}{4}$.

Method 2:

We rewrite $f(x) = x + \sqrt{3-x}$ as $y = x + \sqrt{3-x}$ or $y - x = \sqrt{3-x}$.

Squaring both sides we get: $(y-x)^2 = 3 - x \Rightarrow x^2 - (2y-1)x + y^2 - 3 = 0$.

We know that x is a real number, $\Delta \geq 0$. So $[-(2y-1)]^2 - 4 \times 1 \times (y^2 - 3) \geq 0 \Rightarrow$

$4y^2 + 1 - 4y - 4y^2 + 12 \geq 0 \Rightarrow y \leq \frac{13}{4}$.

The greatest value for y is $\frac{13}{4}$, which occurs when $x = 11/4$.

Problem 4: Solution: 297.

By the divisibility rule for 7, we know that if the positive difference of the last three digits and the rest of the digits is divisible by 7, then the number is divisibly by 7.

$666666 \div 7 = 95238$.

We know that $66 = 11 \times 6$. Thus the quotient will be $\underline{095238}$ $\underline{095238}$······$\underline{095238.}$

The answer is $(9 + 5 + 2 + 3 + 8) \times 11 = 297$.

Problem 5: Solution: 8.

Let the number of weights on the left pan be x and the number of weights on the right pan be y.

We have $5x - 3y = 1$ or $5x - 3y = -1$ with $0 \leq x \leq 20$, and $0 \leq y \leq 20$.

If $5x - 3y = 1$, we have 4 ways:

x	2	5	8	11	14	17
y	3	8	13	18	--	--

If $5x - 3y = -1$, we have 4 ways:

x	1	4	7	10	13	16
y	2	7	12	17	--	--

Total we have 4 + 4 = 8 ways.

Problem 6: Solution: $\dfrac{144}{13}$.

As shown in the figure, $\triangle DCG \sim \triangle GBH \sim \triangle AFH$. $\triangle DCG$ is a 5-12-13 right triangle. $BG = 12 - 5 = 7$.

$\dfrac{GH}{BG} = \dfrac{13}{12} \Rightarrow GH = \dfrac{13}{12} \times 7 = \dfrac{91}{12}$. Thus $HB = \sqrt{GH^2 - 7^2} = \dfrac{35}{12}$

$\dfrac{FH}{AH} = \dfrac{HB}{GH} \Rightarrow \dfrac{FH}{AB - HB} = \dfrac{HB}{GH} \Rightarrow \Rightarrow \dfrac{FH}{12 - HB} = \dfrac{HB}{GH}$

$\Rightarrow FH = \dfrac{HB}{GH} \times (12 - HB) = \dfrac{\frac{35}{12}}{\frac{91}{12}} \times (12 - \dfrac{35}{12}) = \dfrac{545}{156}$. So $GH + FH = \dfrac{91}{12} + \dfrac{545}{156} = \dfrac{144}{13}$.

Problem 7: Solution: 123.

The last term in nth row is n^2.

$44^2 = 1936 < 2014 < 45^2 = 2025$. The last term is 44th row is 1936. $2014 - 1936 = 78$.

2014 is in the 45 row and 78 column $\Rightarrow n + m = 45 + 78 = 123$.

Problem 8: Solution: 27.

Let the six numbers on the faces of the cube be a, b, c, d, e, and f, respectively and $2 \leq a, b, c, d, e, f \leq 15$.

The sum of the 8 numbers in the vertices can be written as

$a(cd + de + ef + fc) + b(cd + de + ef + fc)$
$= (cd + de + ef + fc)(a + b) = [d(c + e) + f(e + c)](a + b) = (c + e)(d + f)(a + b) = 585 = 3 \times 13 \times 15 = 5 \times 9 \times 13 = 3 \times 5 \times 39$.

Since $2 \leq a, b, c, d, e, f \leq 15$, only $(c + e)(d + f)(a + b) = 5 \times 9 \times 13$ is possible.

Therefore $a + b + c + d + e + f = 5 + 9 + 13 = 27$.

Twenty Mathcounts Target Round Tests   Test 17

MATHCOUNTS

■ Mock Competition Seventeen ■

Target Round

Name _____

State _____

DO NOT BEGIN UNTIL YOU ARE INSTRUCTED TO DO SO.

This section of the competition consists of eight problems, which will be presented in pairs. Work on one pair of problems will be completed and answers will be collected before the next pair is distributed. The time limit for each pair of problems is six minutes. The first pair of problems is on the other side of this sheet. When told to do so, turn the page over and begin working. Record only final answers in the designated blanks on the problem sheet. All answers must be complete, legible, and simplified to lowest terms. This round assumes the use of calculators, and calculations may also be done on scratch paper, but no other aids are allowed. If you complete the problems before time is called, use the time remaining to check your answers.

Total Correct	Scorer's Initials

Copyright   MYMATHCOUNTS.COM. All rights reserved.

Twenty Mathcounts Target Round Tests   **Test 17**

1. _____ A state had two letters followed by four digits as the format for license plates. In order to increase the number of plates available, the state changed the format to three letters followed by three digits. What is the positive difference between the number of plates available with the new format and the number of plates available with the old format?

2. _____ Two regular square pyramids have all edges 24 cm in length. The pyramids have parallel bases and parallel edges, and each has a vertex at the center of the other pyramid's base. What is the total number of cubic centimeters in the volume of the solid of intersection of the two pyramids? Express your answer in simplest radical form.

Twenty Mathcounts Target Round Tests   Test 17

3. _____ The variables a, b, c, d, e and f each represent exactly one of the integers 1 through 6. Given the following facts, which integer is represented by e?

$$a + b = c$$
$$b + c = d$$
$$e + c = f$$

4. _____ A sequence of letters is formed by writing 1 A, 2 B's, 3 C's, and so forth, increasing the number of letters written by one each time the next letter of the alphabet is written. What is the 284th letter in the sequence?

Twenty Mathcounts Target Round Tests Test 17

5. _____ What is the number of square centimeters in the area of the quadrilateral of integral lengths of all sides?

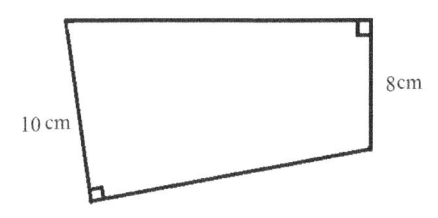

6. _____ In a patio, the pattern is determined by one regular hexagonal tile, six congruent square tiles and six congruent equilateral triangular tiles as shown in the diagram. If the area of the hexagonal tile is $10\sqrt{3}$ in^2, what is the number of square inches in the total area of the figure? Express your answer to the nearest whole number.

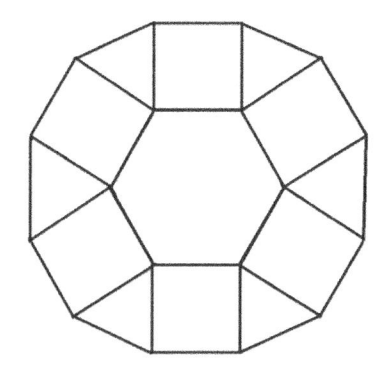

7. _____ What is the sum of all whole numbers from 1 to 2015 that are perfect squares or perfect cubes?

8. _____ Alex selected an even positive integer from 1 to 10, and Bob selected an odd positive integer from 1 to 15. What is the probability that the number selected by Bob is greater than the number selected by Alex? Express your answer as a common fraction.

Twenty Mathcounts Target Round Tests   Test 17

SOLUTIONS:

Problem 1: Solution: 10816000.

The number of plates available before changing:

L, L, N, N, N, N: $26 \times 26 \times 10 \times 10 \times 10 \times 10 = 6760000$.

The number of plates available after changing:

L, L, L, N, N, N: $26 \times 26 \times 26 \times 10 \times 10 \times 10 = 17576000$.

The difference is $17576000 - 6760000 = 10816000$.

Problem 2: Solution: $576\sqrt{2}$.

We draw the figure as follows. We see that the solid of intersection of the two pyramids is an octahedron or two smaller pyramids having all edges 12 cm in length.

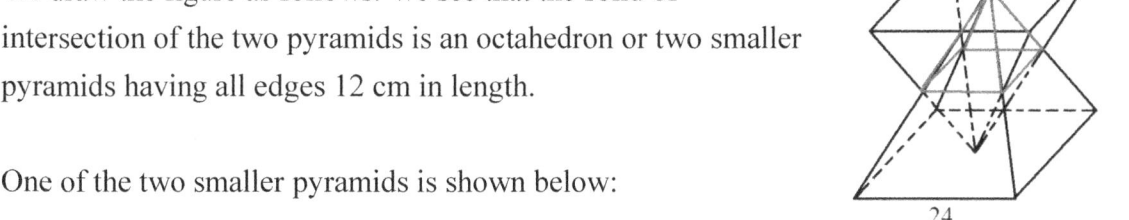

One of the two smaller pyramids is shown below:

Applying Pythagorean Theorem to right triangle ABC:

$$AC = \sqrt{AB^2 - BC^2} = \sqrt{12^2 - 6^2} = 6\sqrt{3}.$$

Applying Pythagorean Theorem to right triangle ADC:

$$AD = \sqrt{AC^2 - BC^2} = \sqrt{(6\sqrt{3})^2 - 6^2} = 6\sqrt{2}.$$

The volume is $\frac{1}{3} \times 12 \times 12 \times 6\sqrt{2} = 288\sqrt{2}$

The answer is $2 \times 288\sqrt{2} = 576\sqrt{2}$.

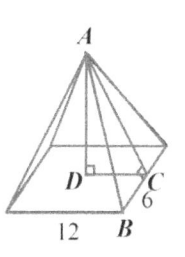

Problem 3: Solution: 2.

Method 1:

We know that $a + b = c$, so c is greater than a or b.

We know that $b + c = d$ and $e + c = f$, so d and f are the digits 5 and 6, not necessarily in that order.

So we can have the following figure:

147

Twenty Mathcounts Target Round Tests   **Test 17**

```
□       5
□    c
□       6
```

c is neither 1 or 2. c can only be 4 since only $3 + 3 = 6$. So we have

```
1       5
2    4
3       6
```

We see that $2 + 4 = 6$. Thus $e = 2$.

Method 2:
$a + b + c + d + e + f = 21$ (1)

We know that $a + b = c$, so c is greater than a or b.

We know that $b + c = d$ and $e + c = f$, so d and f are the digits 5 and 6, not necessarily in that order.

Thus $d + f = 11$ (2)

Substituting (2) into (1):

$a + b + c + e = 10$ (3)

or $2c + e = 10$ (4)

The only value for c is 4, while $e = 2$.
($f = e + c = 2 + 4 = 6$, $b = d - c = 5 - 4 = 1$, and $a = c - b = 4 - 1 = 3$).

Problem 4: Solution: x.

$1 + 2 + 3 + \ldots + n = \dfrac{n(n+1)}{2}$.

We know that $\dfrac{23(23+1)}{2} = 276 < 284 < \dfrac{24(24+1)}{2} = 300$.

So 284 is the $n = 24^{\text{th}}$ letter. 26th letter is z and 25th letter is y. So 24th letter is x.

Problem 5: Solution: 80.

We connect the diagonal and label the two sides a and b as shown in the figure below.

By Pythagorean Theorem, we have $10^2 + a^2 = 8^2 + b^2 \Rightarrow b^2 - a^2 = 36 \Rightarrow (b-a)(b+a) = 36$.

We know that $b - a$ and $b + a$ have the same parity.
So we can only have
$$\begin{cases} b - a = 2 \\ b + a = 18 \end{cases}$$
Solving we get $a = 8$ and $b = 10$.
The area of the quadrilateral is $8 \times 10 = 80$.

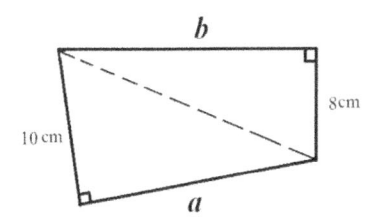

Problem 6: Solution: 75.

The hexagon can be divided into six smaller equilateral triangles as shown.

The area of each smaller equilateral is $\dfrac{a^2}{4}\sqrt{3}$, where a is the length of each side.

Since the area of the hexagon is $10\sqrt{3}$, we have

$6 \times \dfrac{a^2}{4}\sqrt{3} = 10\sqrt{3} \quad \Rightarrow \quad 3a^2 = 20.$

The total area of the figure will be the sum of the areas of 12 equilateral triangles and 6 squares.

$12 \times \dfrac{a^2}{4}\sqrt{3} + 6a^2 = 3a^2(\sqrt{3} + 2) = 20(\sqrt{3} + 2) \approx 75.$

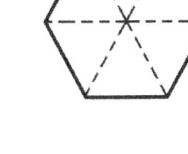

Problem 7: Solution: 34660.

There are $\lfloor \sqrt{2015} \rfloor = 44$ perfect squares and $\lfloor \sqrt[3]{2015} \rfloor = 12$ perfect cubes

We know that $1^2 + 2^2 + \ldots + n^2 = \dfrac{1}{6}n(n+1)(2n+1)$.

Thus the sum of all these perfect square numbers is $= \dfrac{1}{6} \times 44 \times (44+1)(2 \times 44 + 1) = 29370$.

Twenty Mathcounts Target Round Tests — Test 17

We also know that $1^3 + 2^3 + \ldots + n^3 = [\frac{1}{2}n(n+1)]^2$.

Thus the sum of all these perfect cubes is $[\frac{1}{2} \times 12(12+1)]^2 = 6084$.

There are $\lfloor 2 \times \sqrt[3]{2015} \rfloor = 3$ numbers that are both perfect squares and perfect cubes: 1^3, 8^2, and 9^3 that we counted twice.

So the answer is $29370 + 6084 - (1^3 + 8^2 + 9^3) = 34660$.

Problem 8: Solution: $\frac{5}{8}$.

Say that Alex picks up a number from the set $\{2, 4, 6, 8, 10\}$ and Bob picks up a number from the set $\{1, 3, 5, 7, 9, 11, 13, 15\}$.

Let B be the event that the number selected by Bob is greater than the number selected by Alex.

A_1 be the event that Alex picks up the number 2,
B_1 be the event that Bob picks up a number that is larger than Alex's number after A_1
A_2 be the event that Alex picks up the number 4,
B_2 be the event that Bob picks up a number that is larger than Alex's number after A_2
A_3 be the event that Alex picks up the number 6,
B_3 be the event that Bob picks up a number that is larger than Alex's number after A_3
A_4 be the event that Alex picks up the number 8,
B_4 be the event that Bob picks up a number that is larger than Alex's number after A_4
A_5 be the event that Alex picks up the number 10, and
B_5 be the event that Bob picks up a number that is larger than Alex's number after A_5.

By the law of total probability: $B = A_1B_1 + A_2B_2 + A_3B_3 + A_4B_4 + A_5B_5$

$P(B) = P(A_1B_1) + P(A_2B_2) + P(A_3B_3) + P(A_4B_4) + P(A_5B_5)$
$= P(A_1)P(B_1|A_1) + P(A_2)P(B_2|A_2) + P(A_3)P(B_3|A_3) + P(A_4)P(B_4|A_4) + P(A_5)(B_5|A_5)$

Or $P(B) = \frac{1}{5} \times \frac{7}{8} + \frac{1}{5} \times \frac{6}{8} + \frac{1}{5} \times \frac{5}{8} + \frac{1}{5} \times \frac{4}{8} + \frac{1}{5} \times \frac{3}{8} = \frac{1}{5} \times \frac{25}{8} = \frac{5}{8}$.

MATHCOUNTS

■ **Mock Competition Eighteen** ■

Target Round

Name _____

State _____

DO NOT BEGIN UNTIL YOU ARE INSTRUCTED TO DO SO.

This section of the competition consists of eight problems, which will be presented in pairs. Work on one pair of problems will be completed and answers will be collected before the next pair is distributed. The time limit for each pair of problems is six minutes. The first pair of problems is on the other side of this sheet. When told to do so, turn the page over and begin working. Record only final answers in the designated blanks on the problem sheet. All answers must be complete, legible, and simplified to lowest terms. This round assumes the use of calculators, and calculations may also be done on scratch paper, but no other aids are allowed. If you complete the problems before time is called, use the time remaining to check your answers.

Total Correct	Scorer's Initials

Copyright MYMATHCOUNTS.COM. All rights reserved.

Twenty Mathcounts Target Round Tests Test 18

1. _____ When 1108, 1453, 1844, and 2281 are divided by a positive integer n, the remainders are the same. What is the remainder when 29 is divided by n? $n > 1$.

2. _____ The length of the side of the rhombus $ABCD$ is 16. Find the area of the inscribed square $EFGH$ if $\angle ABC = 60°$. Express your answer to the nearest integer.

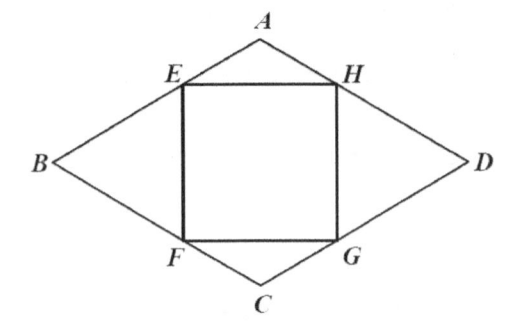

Twenty Mathcounts Target Round Tests Test 18

3. _____ If $\dfrac{1}{a} - \dfrac{1}{b} = \dfrac{1}{a+b}$, find the value of $(\dfrac{b}{a})^2 + (\dfrac{a}{b})^2$.

4. _____ A gardener plants eight trees of three kinds out of three maple trees, two oak trees, and four birch trees in a row. How many ways are there?

5. _____ △PQR is an equilateral triangle. Points A, B, and D are on PQ, QR, RP, respectively. ABCDE is a regular pentagon with ∠PDE= 30°. Find ∠CBR.

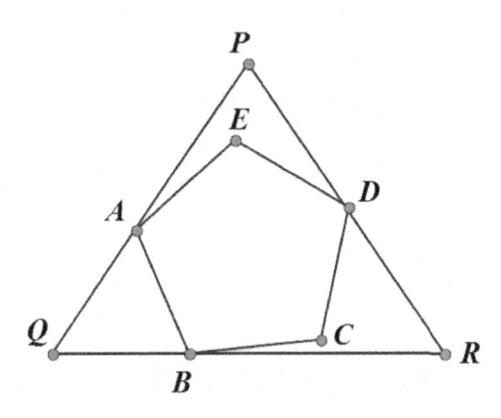

6. _____ Seven distinct gifts are given to 2 children, with each person having at least two gifts. How many ways are there?

7. _____ Find the number of integer solutions to the inequality: $|x-7|+|x| \leq 21$.

8. _____ Three girls and 4 boys are seating around a circular table. There must be at least a boy between any two girls. How many different ways of seating are there?

Twenty Mathcounts Target Round Tests   **Test 18**

SOLUTIONS:

Problem 1: Solution: 6.
Method 1:
$1108 = nq_1 + r$ \hfill (1)
$1453 = nq_2 + r$ \hfill (2)
$1844 = nq_3 + r$ \hfill (3)
$2281 = nq_4 + r$ \hfill (4)
(3) – (2): $391 = n(q_3 - q_2)$ $\Rightarrow$ $n(q_3 - q_2), = 23 \times 17$.
Since 23 and 17 are prime numbers, n must be either 23 or 17.
(4) – (3): $437 = n(q_4 - q_3)$ $\Rightarrow$ $n(q_4 - q_3) = 23 \times 19$.
Thus n is 23. $29 = 23 + 6$.
The remainder when 29 is divided by n is 6.

Method 2:
$1108 \equiv r$ \quad (mod n) \hfill (1)
$1453 \equiv r$ \quad (mod n) \hfill (2)
$1844 \equiv r$ \quad (mod n) \hfill (3)
$2281 \equiv r$ \quad (mod n) \hfill (4)
(3) – (2):
$391 \equiv 0$ \quad (mod n) \hfill (5)
$391 = 23 \times 17$.
(5) means that n is divisible by 23 or 17. Since both 23 and 17 are prime numbers, n can be either 23 or 17.
(4) – (3): $437 \equiv 0$ \quad (mod n) \hfill (6)
$437 = 23 \times 19$.
Thus n is 23. $29 = 23 + 6$.
The remainder when 29 is divided by n is 6.

Problem 2: Solution: 103.
We connect AC and BD and label K, M and N as shown in the figure. Let $KE = x$.

156

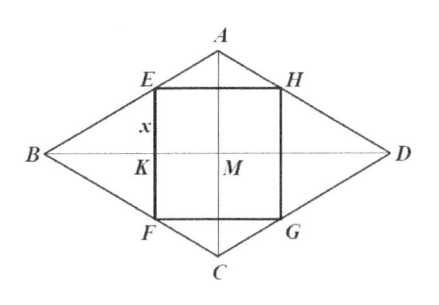

We see that $AM = \frac{1}{2}AB = 8$, and

$BM = \sqrt{16^2 - 8^2} = 8\sqrt{3}$. $\triangle ABM \sim \triangle BKE$.

$\dfrac{BM}{AM} = \dfrac{BK}{KE} \Rightarrow \dfrac{8\sqrt{3}}{8} = \dfrac{8\sqrt{3} - x}{x} \Rightarrow$

$\sqrt{3}x = 8\sqrt{3} - x \Rightarrow (\sqrt{3}+1)x = 8\sqrt{3} \Rightarrow x = \dfrac{8\sqrt{3}}{(\sqrt{3}+1)}$.

The area of the square is $4x^2$. Thus $4x^2 = 4 \times \left(\dfrac{8\sqrt{3}}{(\sqrt{3}+1)}\right)^2 \approx 102.89 = 103$

Problem 3: Solution: 3.

$\dfrac{1}{a} - \dfrac{1}{b} = \dfrac{1}{a+b} \Rightarrow \dfrac{b-a}{ab} = \dfrac{1}{a+b} \Rightarrow b^2 - a^2 = ab$

$\left(\dfrac{b}{a}\right)^2 + \left(\dfrac{a}{b}\right)^2 = \dfrac{b^4 + a^4}{a^2 b^2} = \dfrac{(b^2-a^2)^2 + 2a^2 b^2}{a^2 b^2} = \dfrac{a^2 b^2 + 2a^2 b^2}{a^2 b^2} = 3$.

Problem 4: Solution: 1260.

Case I: With two maple trees, two oak trees, and four birch trees, by (3.1), we have

$\dfrac{8!}{2!2!4!} = 420$ ways.

Case II: With three maple trees, one oak tree, and four birch trees, there are

$\dfrac{8!}{3!1!4!} = 280$ ways.

Case III: With three maple trees, two oak trees, and three birch trees, there are

$\dfrac{8!}{3!2!3!} = 560$ ways.

By the sum rule, we know that the total number of ways to plant the trees is
$420 + 280 + 560 = 1260$.

Twenty Mathcounts Target Round Tests — Test 18

Problem 5: Solution: 6.

Method 1:

We label some known angles as follows:

We know that $\angle AED = \angle PAE + \angle PDE + \angle P \Rightarrow$
$108 = \angle PAE + 30 + 60 \Rightarrow \angle PAE = 18°$.

Thus $\angle QAB = 180 - 108 - 18 = 54$, and

$\angle QBA = 180 - 60 - 54 = 66$.

Then $\angle CBR = 180 - 66 - 108 = 6°$.

Method 2:

$\angle EDC = \angle DCB = 108°, \angle CDR = 180° - 108° - 30° = 42°$.

Connect DB.

$\angle CBD = \angle CDB = (180° - 108°) \div 2 = 36°$.

$\angle R = 60° \Rightarrow \angle CBR = 180° - 60° - 42° - 36° - 36° = 6°$

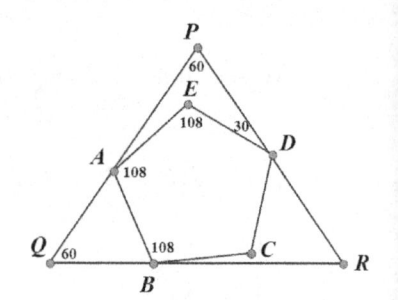

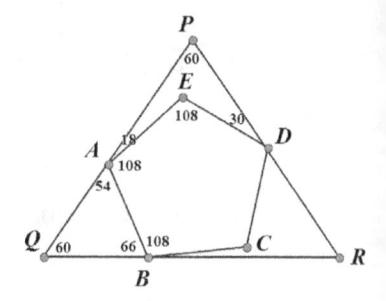

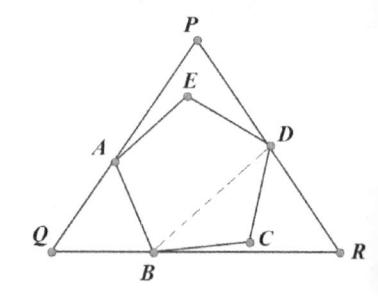

Problem 6: Solution: 112.

Method 1:

Each gift has two ways to be given out: to child A or to child B. For 7 gifts, the number of ways to be given out: $2 \times 2 \times 2 \times 2 \times 2 \times 2 \times 2 = 128$.

Among 128 ways, there are two cases not satisfying the condition:

(1) child A gets 7 gifts and child B gets 0 gift; child B gets 7 gifts and child A gets 0 gift).
There are 2 ways; and

(2) child A gets 6 gifts and child B gets 1 gift; child B gets 6 gifts and child A gets 1 gift).

There are $\binom{7}{6} \times \binom{1}{1} \times 2 = 14$ ways.

The answer is $128 - 2 - 14 = 112$.

Method 2:

We have two cases:

Case 1: $7 = 5 + 2$.

$$\binom{7}{2} \times \binom{2}{2} \times 2 = 42$$

Case 2: 7 = 4 + 3.

$$\binom{7}{4} \times \binom{3}{3} \times 2 = 70.$$

The total ways are 42 + 70 = 112.

Problem 7: Solution: 22.

$|x-7| + |x| \leq 21$

We have three cases:

Case 1: $x < 0$.

$-x + 7 - x \leq 21 \Rightarrow x \geq -7 \Rightarrow x = -7, -6, -5, -4, -3, -2, -1$. We get 7 solutions

Case 2: $0 \leq x \leq 7$

$-x + 7 + x \leq 21 \quad \Rightarrow \quad 7 \leq 21$. No matter what value of x, the inequality is still satisfied. So we have 8 solutions (0, 1, 2, 3, 4, 5, 6, 7).

Case 3: $x > 7$.

$x \geq 7 \quad \Rightarrow \quad x - 7 + x \leq 21 \quad \Rightarrow \quad x \leq 14 \quad \Rightarrow x = 14, 13, 12, 11, 10, 9, 8$. So we have 7 solutions.

The answer is 7 + 8 + 7 = 22.

Problem 8: Solution: 144.

First let every girl choose her neighbor.

Girl 1 can choose one of the 4 boys.

Girl 2 can choose one of the 3 boys left.

Girl 3 can choose one of the 2 boys remaining.

There will be three groups and one boy left. This boy is also treated as a group.

So there are 4 groups seating around a circular table and the ways to seat is (4 − 1)!.

Thus the answer is 4 × 3 × 2 × (4 − 1)! = 144 ways.

Twenty Mathcounts Target Round Tests Test 19

MATHCOUNTS

■ Mock Competition Nineteen ■

Target Round

Name _____

State _____

DO NOT BEGIN UNTIL YOU ARE INSTRUCTED TO DO SO.

This section of the competition consists of eight problems, which will be presented in pairs. Work on one pair of problems will be completed and answers will be collected before the next pair is distributed. The time limit for each pair of problems is six minutes. The first pair of problems is on the other side of this sheet. When told to do so, turn the page over and begin working. Record only final answers in the designated blanks on the problem sheet. All answers must be complete, legible, and simplified to lowest terms. This round assumes the use of calculators, and calculations may also be done on scratch paper, but no other aids are allowed. If you complete the problems before time is called, use the time remaining to check your answers.

Total Correct	Scorer's Initials

Copyright   MYMATHCOUNTS.COM. All rights reserved.

Twenty Mathcounts Target Round Tests Test 19

1. _____ In a plane, 11 lines intersect such that no 3 lines meet at the same point. What is the maximum number of regions created by the lines?

2. _____ Right $\triangle ABC$ has legs measuring 8 cm and 15 cm. The triangle is rotated about one of its legs. What is the number of cubic centimeters in the positive difference of the maximum and minimum volumes of the resulting solid? Express your answer in terms of π.

Twenty Mathcounts Target Round Tests Test 19

3. _____ The lengths of the diagonals of a rhombus are 12 inches and 16 inches. If a circle is inscribed in the rhombus, how many inches are in its circumference? Use 3.14 as an approximation for π, and express your answer as a decimal to the nearest tenth.

4. _____ Regular hexagons are placed side-by-side in continuous pattern. What is the maximum number of congruent hexagons that can be placed side-by-side such that the perimeter of the resulting figure is less than 1000 cm?

162

Twenty Mathcounts Target Round Tests **Test 19**

5. _____ At each stage, a new square is drawn on each side of the perimeter of the figure in the previous stage. How many unit squares will be in Stage 11?

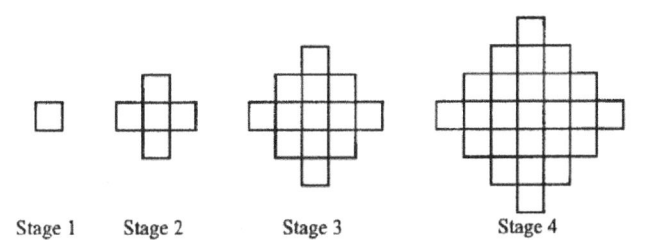

Stage 1   Stage 2   Stage 3   Stage 4

6. _____ Each day, Mr. Mathis divides evenly his 20 students into 5 groups. What is the probability that Alex, Bob, Charles, and Danny will be in the same group today? Express your answer as a common fraction.

163

Twenty Mathcounts Target Round Tests   Test 19

7. _____ A sequence of numbers $a_1, a_2, a_3, \ldots$ is defined by $a_1 = 7$, $a_2 = -6$ and $a_n = a_{n-1} - a_{n-2}$ for $n > 2$. What is the sum of the first 2015 terms of the sequence?

8. _____ In the first two-mile race, Alex beat Bob by $\frac{1}{3}$-mile, and in the second two-mile race, Bob beat Charles by $\frac{1}{2}$-mile. If Alex and Charles run a third two-mile race, and all three runners run at the constant speed in every race, by how many miles will Alex beat Charles? Express your answer as a common fraction.

Twenty Mathcounts Target Round Tests — Test 19

SOLUTIONS:

Problem 1: Solution: 67.

Maximum number of regions n lines can divide a plane is N and

$$N = \binom{n}{0} + \binom{n}{1} + \binom{n}{2} = \frac{n(n+1)}{2} + 1 = \frac{11(11+1)}{2} + 1 = 66 + 1 = 67.$$

Problem 2: Solution: 280π.

We rotate the triangle along the side AC to get the minimum volume:

$$\frac{\pi r^2 h}{3} = \frac{\pi \times 8^2 \times 15}{3} = 320\pi.$$

We then rotate the triangle along the side BC to get the maximum volume:

$$\frac{\pi r^2 h}{3} = \frac{\pi \times 15^2 \times 8}{3} = 600\pi.$$

The positive difference is $600\pi - 320\pi = 280\pi$.

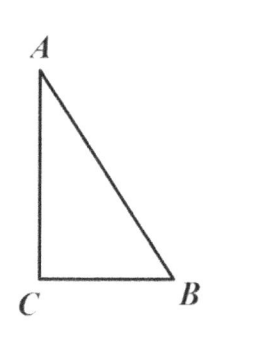

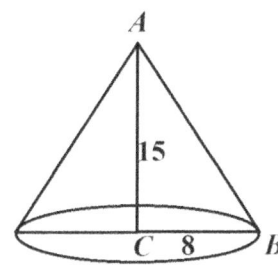

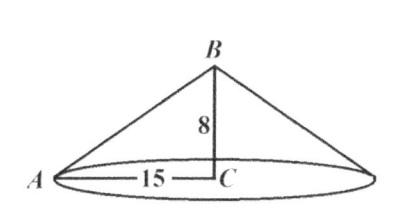

Problem 3: Solution: 30.1.

Method 1:

From the figure below we see that in triangle AOD, $DO = 6$, $AO = 8$, $AD = 10$.

Let $AE = a$ and $ED = b$. $a + b = 10$. EO is the radius r.

Applying Pythagorean Theorem twice to triangles AOE and DOE:

$AO^2 - r^2 = a^2 \quad \Rightarrow \quad 8^2 - r^2 = a^2$ \hfill (1)

$DO^2 - r^2 = b^2 \quad \Rightarrow \quad 6^2 - r^2 = b^2$ \hfill (2)

(1) – (2): $8^2 - 6^2 = a^2 - b^2$ or $28 = (a+b)(a-b) = 10(a-b) \quad \Rightarrow \quad a - b = 2.8$.

Twenty Mathcounts Target Round Tests   Test 19

So $a = 6.4$.

From (1), we get $8^2 - 6.4^2 = r^2 \Rightarrow r = 4.8$.

The circumference of the circle is

$2\pi r = 2 \times 3.14 \times 4.8 = 30.144 \approx 30.1$.

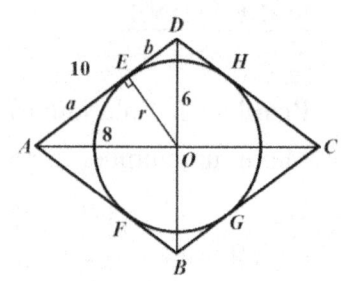

Method 2:

We see that triangles *AOE*, *DOE*, and *AOD* are all right triangles. So we have $AO^2 = AD \times a \Rightarrow 8^2 = 10 \times a \Rightarrow a = 6.4$

Applying Pythagorean Theorem to triangles *AOE* $8^2 - r^2 = a^2 \Rightarrow 8^2 - r^2 = 6.4^2$

$\Rightarrow r = 4.8$

The circumference of the circle is $2\pi r = 2 \times 3.14 \times 4.8 = 30.144 \approx 30.1$.

Method 3:

The area of triangle *AOD* is $\dfrac{1}{2} \times AD \times OD = \dfrac{1}{2} \times 8 \times 6 = 24$.

The area of triangle *AOD* can also be calculated as $\dfrac{1}{2} \times AD \times OE = \dfrac{1}{2} \times 10 \times r = 24$

$5r = 24 \Rightarrow r = 4.8$

The circumference of the circle is $2\pi r = 2 \times 3.14 \times 4.8 = 30.144 \approx 30.1$.

Problem 4: Solution: 143.

We calculate the side length of one hexagon first.

$\angle ABC = 30°$. So $AB = 2AC = 2x$.

Applying Pythagorean Theorem to triangle *ABC*:

$AB^2 - AC^2 = CB^2 \Rightarrow (2x)^2 - x^2 = (\dfrac{3}{2})^2$

So the length of the each side is $2x = \sqrt{3}$.

When we have only one hexagon, we get the length of the sides $6\sqrt{3}$.

When we put two hexagons together, we lost two sides:

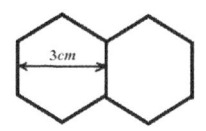

Twenty Mathcounts Target Round Tests   **Test 19**

When we put three hexagons together, we lost four sides:

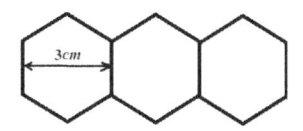

We see the pattern and the sum of the length of the sides of *n* hexagons can be written as:

$L = n \times 6\sqrt{3} - (n-1)(2\sqrt{3})$.

Solving for n: $n = \dfrac{L - 2\sqrt{3}}{4\sqrt{3}}$.

For our case, $L < 1000$. So $n < \dfrac{1000 - 2\sqrt{3}}{4\sqrt{3}} \approx 143.84$.

The maximum number of congruent hexagons is 143.

Problem 5: Solution: 221.

We see the pattern from the figure.

By Newton's Little Formula,

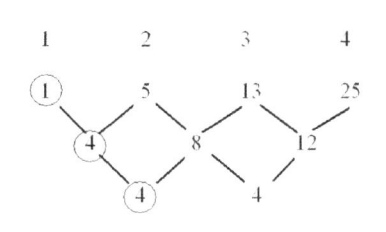

$a_{11} = \dbinom{11-1}{0} + 4\dbinom{11-1}{1} + 4\dbinom{11-1}{2}$

$= 1 + 4 \times 10 + 4 \times 45 = 221$.

Problem 6: Solution: $\dfrac{1}{969}$.

Method 1:

Suppose Alex is already in the group, then there are three spots and 19 students left. The chance for Bob, Charles, or Danny to go to that group is 3/19.

After Bob (or Charles or Danny) goes to the group, there are two spots and 18 students left.

The chance Charles or Danny gets into the group will then be 2/18.

After one of Charles and Danny goes to the group, there is one spot and 17 students left.

Twenty Mathcounts Target Round Tests   **Test 19**

The chance for the remaining person (Charles or Danny) to get into the group will then be 1/17.

So the desired solution is the product: $P = 1 \times \dfrac{3}{19} \times \dfrac{2}{18} \times \dfrac{1}{17} = \dfrac{1}{969}$.

Method 2:

The total number of groups that can be formed is $\binom{20}{4}$, which will also be our denominator. The number of ways such that Alex, Bob, Charles, and Danny are in the same group is $\binom{4}{4}$. There are five groups that these four people may be in, so the desired solution is: $\dfrac{\binom{4}{4} \times 5}{\binom{20}{4}} = \dfrac{1}{969}$.

Method 3:

The total ways to divided 20 students into 5 indistinguishable groups:
$$\dfrac{\binom{20}{4}\binom{16}{4}\binom{12}{4}\binom{8}{4}\binom{4}{4}}{5!}$$

The number of favorable ways (Alex, Bob, Charles, and Danny are in the same group and they can be in any of these 5 groups): $\binom{4}{4} \times \dfrac{\binom{16}{4}\binom{12}{4}\binom{8}{4}\binom{4}{4}}{4!}$.

Probability = Favorable Ways/ Total Ways: $\dfrac{5!}{\binom{20}{4} \times 4!} = \dfrac{5}{4845} = \dfrac{1}{969}$.

Method 4:

Suppose Alex is in a group already. What is the probability that he will be matched with Bob, Charles, and Danny?

3 of the other 18 students are randomly chosen to be paired with him. There are $\binom{19}{3} =$ 969 ways that this can be done, and only in one of these ways is Bob, Charles, and Danny with him.

Therefore, the answer is 1/969.

Problem 7: Solution: − 13.

We write out more terms to see if we can find the pattern:

| 7, | −6, | −13, | −7, | 6, | 13, | 7, | −6, | −13,… |

The sequence repeats every 6 terms. The sum of the first 6 terms is 0. $2015 = 6 \times 335 + 5$. Thus the sum of the first 2015 terms is the same as the sum of the first 5 terms. $7 - 6 - 13 - 7 + 6 = -13$.

Problem 8: Solution: 3/4.

Method 1:

We use the continued ratio to solve this problem.

The numbers below are the distance each person runs.

$$A : B = 2 : 5/3$$
$$B : C = 2 : 3/2$$
$$A : B : C = 4 : 10/3 : 5/2$$

When Alex runs 4 miles, he will beat Charles will only run 5/2 miles.

So When Alex runs 2 miles, Charles will only run 5/4 miles.

When Alex runs 2 miles, he will beat Charles by $2 - 5/4 = 3/4$ miles.

Method 2:

Let V_k, V_j, V_m be the speeds of Alex, Bob, and Charles, respectively.

Let x be the distance Alex will beat Charles and t_1, t_2, and t_3 be the times used for three races. $t_1 = \dfrac{2}{V_k}$, $t_2 = \dfrac{2}{V_j}$, and $t_3 = \dfrac{2}{V_k} = t_1$.

Twenty Mathcounts Target Round Tests — Test 19

$$V_k t_1 - V_j t_1 = \frac{1}{3} \quad \Rightarrow \quad 2 - \frac{2V_j}{V_k} = \frac{1}{3} \quad \Rightarrow \quad \frac{V_j}{V_k} = \frac{5}{6} \qquad (1)$$

$$V_j t_2 - V_m t_2 = \frac{1}{2} \quad \Rightarrow \quad 2 - \frac{2V_m}{V_j} = \frac{1}{2} \quad \Rightarrow \quad \frac{V_m}{V_j} = \frac{3}{4} \qquad (2)$$

$$V_k t_3 - V_m t_3 = x \quad \Rightarrow \quad 2 - \frac{2V_m}{V_k} = x \qquad (3)$$

$$(1) \times (2): \quad \frac{V_m}{V_k} = \frac{5}{6} \times \frac{3}{4} = \frac{5}{8} \qquad (4)$$

Substituting (4) into (3): $2 - \dfrac{2 \times 5}{8} = x \quad \Rightarrow \quad x = 2 - \dfrac{5}{4} = \dfrac{3}{4}$.

Twenty Mathcounts Target Round Tests　　　　　　　　　　　Test 20

MATHCOUNTS

■ **Mock Competition Twenty** ■

Target Round

Name _____

State _____

DO NOT BEGIN UNTIL YOU ARE INSTRUCTED TO DO SO.

This section of the competition consists of eight problems, which will be presented in pairs. Work on one pair of problems will be completed and answers will be collected before the next pair is distributed. The time limit for each pair of problems is six minutes. The first pair of problems is on the other side of this sheet. When told to do so, turn the page over and begin working. Record only final answers in the designated blanks on the problem sheet. All answers must be complete, legible, and simplified to lowest terms. This round assumes the use of calculators, and calculations may also be done on scratch paper, but no other aids are allowed. If you complete the problems before time is called, use the time remaining to check your answers.

Total Correct	Scorer's Initials

Copyright   MYMATHCOUNTS.COM. All rights reserved.

Twenty Mathcounts Target Round Tests Test 20

1. _____ Both *x* and *y* are integers. $x + 9y$ is divisible by 5. What is the remainder when $8x + 7y$ is divided by 5?

2. _____ *ABCD* is a rectangle. *E* is a point on *BC* and *F* is a point on *CD*. The areas of the triangles *ABE*, *ECF*, and *FDA* are 4, 3, and 5, respectively. What is the area of the triangle *AEF*?

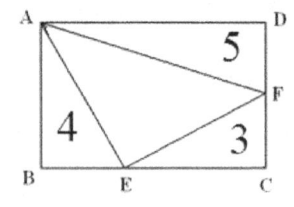

Twenty Mathcounts Target Round Tests　　　　　　　　　　　　**Test 20**

3. _____ Seven identical chairs in a row are to be seated by four students. How many arrangements are there such that the only two of the three empty chairs are next to each other?

4. _____ As shown in the figure, $AB = AC = 17$, $BC = 16$. $BC // DE$. Both O_1 and O_2 are inscribed circles tangent to the DE. Find the ratio of the radius of O_1 to the radius of O_2.

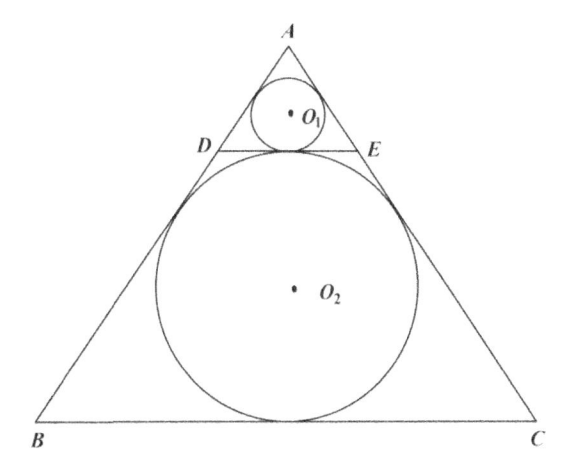

5. _____ Two legs of a trapezoid are 6 and 8. Two bases of the trapezoid are 10 and 20. Find the length of the segment connecting the midpoints of two bases.

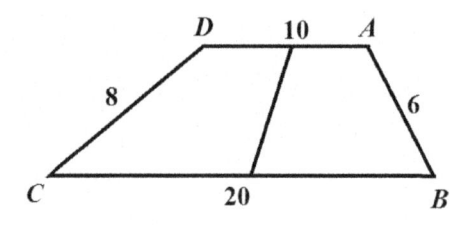

6. _____ Find $a^2+b^2+c^2+ab+bc+ca$ if $a=\sqrt{5}+\sqrt{3}-1$, $b=\sqrt{5}-\sqrt{3}+1$, $c=-\sqrt{5}+\sqrt{3}+1$.

7. _____ The product of two positive integers is 16111 more than sum of them. What is the greater one of these two integers if one of them is a square number?

8. _____ Figure 1 as shown consists of one small square and there is no any 2×2 square in it. Figure 2 consists of three small squares and there is no any 2×2 square in it as well. Figure 3 consists of six small squares and there is one 2×2 square in it.

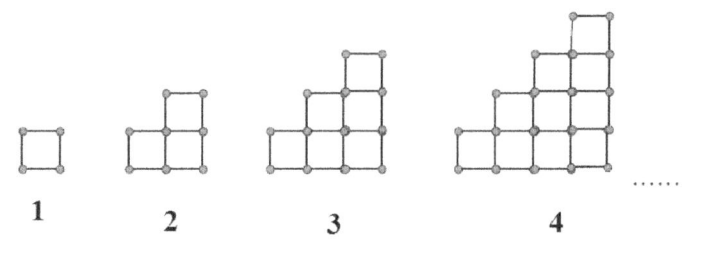

Figure 4 consists of ten small squares and there are three 2×2 squares in it (see figure below).

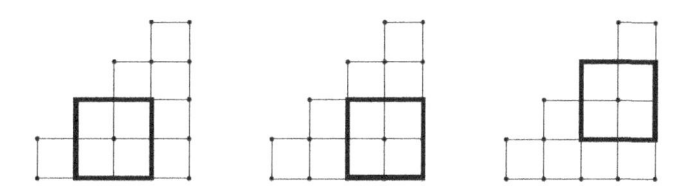

How many 2×2 squares can you count in figure 102 if the pattern continues?

Twenty Mathcounts Target Round Tests   **Test 20**

SOLUTIONS:

Problem 1: Solution: 0.
Method 1:
$8x + 7y = 5(2x + 5y) - 2(x + 9y)$.
Since $x + 9y$ is divisible by 5, the remainder when $8x + 7y$ is divided by 5 is 0.

Method 2:
Let $x = 1$ and $y = 1$. Therefore $x + 9y = 10$ which is divisible by 5.
$8x + 7y = 8 \times 1 + 7 \times 1 = 15$ which is also divisible by 5.
The remainder when $8x + 7y$ is divided by 5 is 0.

Problem 2: Solution: 8.
Method 1:
Let $AD = x$, so $DF = 10/x$
Let $AB = y$, so $BE = 8/y$
Thus $CE = x - 8/y$ and $CF = y - 10/x$. Using $CE \times CF = 6$, we have
$xy + 80/(xy) = 24$.
It follows that $xy = 20$ or 4, but 4 is clearly not feasible. $20 - (4 + 3 + 5) = 8$.

Method 2:
We know that $S_{ABCD} = 2S_{\triangle AEF} + BE \times DF$.
Let the area of the triangle AEF be S.
Then: $3 + 4 + 5 + S = 2S + BE \times DF \quad \Rightarrow \quad 12 = S + \dfrac{BE \times AB}{AB} \times \dfrac{DF \times AD}{AD}$

$\Rightarrow \quad 12 = S + \dfrac{8 \times 10}{12 + S} \quad \Rightarrow S = 8$.

Method 3:
Connect AC. Let $S_{\triangle AEC} = x$ and $S_{\triangle CAF} = y$. We have $x + 4 = y + 5$ or $x = y + 1$

In $\triangle ABC$ and $\triangle AEC$, $\dfrac{x+4}{x} = \dfrac{BC}{EC}$.

176

In $\triangle ACF$ and $\triangle ECF$, $\dfrac{y}{3} = \dfrac{AD}{EC}$.

Since $AD = BC$, $\dfrac{x+4}{x} = \dfrac{y}{3}$.

Solve x and y in (1) and (2): $x = 6$ and $y = 5$.

$S_{\triangle AEF} = x + y - 3 = 8$.

The conclusion is also true if $ABCD$ is a parallelogram.

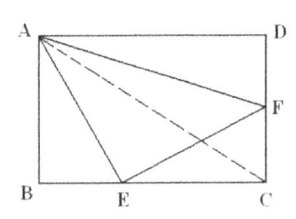

Problem 3: Solution: 480.

We tie the two empty chairs next to each other together and treat them as on unit, namely A. the other empty chair is B.

We have $4! = 24$ ways to sit four students. There are $\binom{5}{2} = 10$ ways to insert A and B.

and we multiply the result by 2 because A and B can switch their positions.

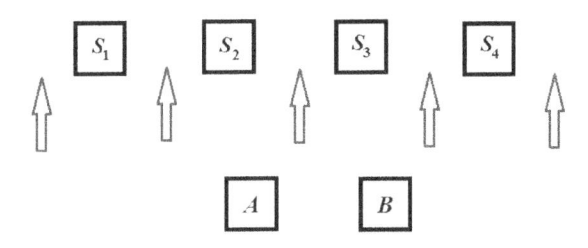

By the product rule, the answer will be $24 \times 10 \times 2 = 480$.

Problem 4: Solution: $\dfrac{9}{25}$.

Method 1:

Draw $\overline{AF} \perp \overline{BC}$ to meet BC at F.

$\overline{BF} = \overline{FC} = 16 \div 2 = 8$. $\overline{AF} = \sqrt{17^2 - 8^2} = 15$.

$BH = BF = 8$. $AH = 17 - 8 = 9$.

We see that $DG = DH$.

The perimeter of $\triangle ADE$ is $P_1 = 9 + 9 = 18$.

The perimeter of $\triangle ABC = P_2 = 17 + 17 + 16 = 50$.

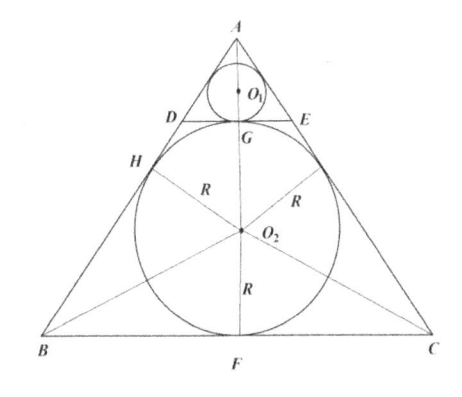

177

$\triangle ADE \sim \triangle ABC \Rightarrow \dfrac{r}{R} = \dfrac{P_1}{P_2} = \dfrac{18}{50} = \dfrac{9}{25}$.

Method 2:

Draw $\overline{AF} \perp \overline{BC}$ to meet BC at F.

$\overline{BF} = \overline{FC} = 16 \div 2 = 8$. $\overline{AF} = \sqrt{17^2 - 8^2} = 15$.

$BH = BF = 8$. $AH = 17 - 8 = 9$.

$\triangle AHO_2 \sim \triangle ABF$, So $\dfrac{AB}{BF} = \dfrac{AO_2}{R} \Rightarrow$

$\dfrac{17}{8} = \dfrac{15 - R}{R} \Rightarrow R = \dfrac{24}{5}$.

$\triangle AKO_1 \sim \triangle ABF$, So $\dfrac{AF}{BF} = \dfrac{AO_1}{r} \Rightarrow$

$\dfrac{17}{8} = \dfrac{15 - 2R - r}{r} \Rightarrow r = \dfrac{216}{125}$.

$\dfrac{r}{R} = \dfrac{216}{125} / \dfrac{24}{5} = \dfrac{9}{25}$.

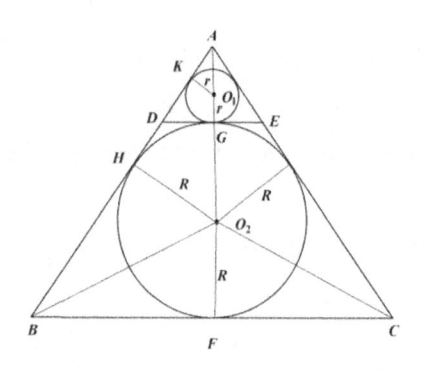

Problem 5: Solution: 5.

Connect DE. Since $DA = BE$, $DABE$ is a parallelogram. So $DE = AB = 6$.

Triangle ADE is a 6-8-10 right triangle so $\angle EDC = 90°$.

Draw $\overline{DF} \perp \overline{EC}$ at $F \Rightarrow \dfrac{10 \times \overline{DF}}{2} = \dfrac{6 \times 8}{2} \Rightarrow \overline{DF} = \dfrac{24}{5}$.

Draw $\overline{EH} \perp \overline{GD}$ at $H \Rightarrow \overline{EH} = \overline{DF} = \dfrac{24}{5}$.

$\overline{DH} = \sqrt{6^2 - (\dfrac{24}{5})^2} = \dfrac{18}{5}$, $\overline{GD} = \dfrac{10}{2} = 5$. $\overline{GH} = 5 - \dfrac{18}{5} = \dfrac{7}{5}$.

$\overline{GE} = \sqrt{(\dfrac{7}{5})^2 + (\dfrac{24}{5})^2} = 5$.

Problem 6: Solution: 18.

$$\frac{1}{2}(2a^2 + 2b^2 + 2c^2 + 2ab + 2bc + 2ac) = \frac{1}{2}[(a+b)^2 + (b+c)^2 + (a+c)^2]$$
$$= \frac{1}{2}[(2\sqrt{5})^2 + 2^2 + (2\sqrt{3})^2] = \frac{1}{2}(20 + 4 + 12) = 18$$

Problem 7: Solution: 2015.

Let two numbers be x, y with $x \geq y$.

$xy = x + y + 16111 \Rightarrow x(y-1) - (y-1) = 16111 + 1 \Rightarrow (x-1)(y-1) = 16112$.

$16112 = 2^4 \times 19 \times 53 = 2^3 \times 2 \times 19 \times 53$

If we let $x - 1 = 2^3$, then $y = 2 \times 19 \times 53 = 2014$. We get $x = 3^2$ and $y = 2015$.

Thus the greater of two numbers is 2015.

Problem 8: Solution: 5050.

We see that pattern

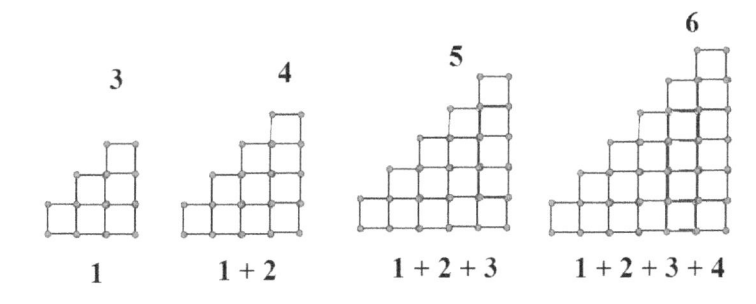

$100 + 99 + 98 + ... + 3 + 2 + 1 = 5050$.

Twenty Mock Mathcounts Target Round Tests — Index

A

acute angle, 91

alternate interior angles, 70

angle, 95, 96

arc, 64

area, 2, 5, 6, 8, 16, 19, 23, 42, 48, 55, 76, 91, 92, 97, 100, 101, 103, 112, 125, 129, 139, 145, 149, 152, 157, 166, 172, 176

arithmetic mean, 126, 129

arithmetic sequence, 28, 83, 101, 104, 105

B

base, 11, 143

C

center, 39, 48, 64, 68, 143

circle, 5, 8, 12, 16, 23, 29, 39, 48, 55, 59, 64, 66, 68, 72, 78, 81, 91, 95, 102, 106, 125, 128, 129, 133, 162, 166

circumference, 78, 91, 128, 162, 166

collinear, 91

combination, 26

common divisor, 37, 41

common factor, 103

common fraction, 22, 47, 57, 146, 163, 164

cone, 75, 77

congruent, 4, 70, 72, 75, 110, 112, 121, 125, 162, 167

constant, 73

counting, 138

cube, 22, 25, 56, 93, 119, 127, 130, 138, 141

cylinder, 77

D

data, 126

decimal, 3, 19, 31, 39, 109, 110, 125, 126, 162

denominator, 168

diagonal, 129, 149

diameter, 12, 16, 55, 66, 129

difference, 23, 30, 46, 83, 92, 97, 140, 143, 147, 161, 165

digit, 13, 14, 17, 21, 23, 24, 30, 37, 39, 40, 43, 65, 82, 86, 87, 90, 117, 121, 127, 131, 136

divisible, 20, 21, 23, 24, 65, 68, 69, 82, 86, 87, 140, 156, 172, 176

divisor, 17, 43

E

equation, 41, 44, 69, 114, 131

equilateral, 2, 6, 11, 30, 70, 76, 145, 149, 154

equilateral triangle, 2, 6, 11, 30, 70, 76, 149, 154

even number, 17

event, 42, 150

F

face, 22, 25, 56, 59, 119, 122, 138

factor, 86, 87, 107

formula, 139

fraction, 2, 65, 68, 73, 76, 126

function, 5, 72

Twenty Mock Mathcounts Target Round Tests — Index

G

geometric sequence, 28, 32

H

hexagon, 149, 166

I

inequality, 24, 155, 159

integer, 4, 5, 11, 30, 39, 40, 41, 43, 49, 50, 56, 64, 82, 86, 88, 93, 131, 138, 144, 146, 152, 155

integers, 5, 11, 41, 46, 47, 48, 51, 72, 76, 80, 82, 102, 103, 109, 111, 113, 118, 121, 128, 138, 144, 172, 175

intersection, 66, 143, 147

isosceles, 40, 43, 58, 61, 62, 70

isosceles triangle, 58, 61, 62, 70

L

least common multiple, 23, 103, 120

line, 3, 6, 68, 120

line segment, 6

lowest terms, 1, 10, 18, 27, 36, 45, 54, 63, 71, 79, 89, 99, 108, 115, 124, 134, 142, 151, 160, 171

M

mean, 74, 77, 78

median, 120

midpoint, 3, 28, 68, 70, 116

multiple, 12, 51, 68, 86, 93

N

natural number, 13, 20, 126

natural numbers, 126

O

octahedron, 147

odd number, 13

ordered pair, 111

P

parallel, 70, 143

parallelogram, 67, 177, 178

pentagon, 96, 110, 154

percent, 91

perimeter, 2, 4, 6, 8, 53, 125, 129, 162, 163, 177

perpendicular, 103, 128

plane, 161, 165

point, 7, 39, 48, 67, 80, 83, 88, 161, 172

polygon, 8

positive number, 28, 117

prime number, 50, 55, 59, 156

probability, 2, 3, 6, 22, 26, 31, 35, 38, 39, 42, 47, 51, 57, 60, 126, 130, 146, 150, 163, 168

product, 22, 26, 90, 94, 117, 138, 168, 175, 177

proportion, 76

pyramid, 11, 15, 143

Pythagorean Theorem, 8, 16, 32, 44, 52, 69, 78, 84, 85, 129, 133, 139, 147, 149, 165, 166

Q

quadrilateral, 74, 77, 91, 100, 145, 149

Twenty Mock Mathcounts Target Round Tests — Index

quotient, 14, 17, 64, 136, 140

R

radius, 5, 29, 39, 48, 59, 72, 75, 77, 92, 102, 106, 125, 133, 165, 173

random, 2, 31, 39, 47

rate, 41, 73

ratio, 2, 6, 42, 59, 95, 125, 128, 129, 133, 169, 173

real number, 66, 73, 136, 140

real numbers, 66, 73

rectangle, 5, 8, 12, 16, 29, 66, 80, 112, 125, 129, 137, 139, 172

regular polygon, 4

relatively prime, 48, 107

remainder, 4, 8, 13, 15, 17, 39, 40, 43, 152, 156, 172, 176

rhombus, 152, 162

right triangle, 8, 16, 69, 84, 85, 120, 141, 147, 166, 178

rotation, 77

S

sequence, 104, 123, 144, 164, 169

set, 41, 73, 113, 121, 126, 150

similar, 4, 113

solution, 32, 41, 132, 139, 168

square, 5, 8, 9, 11, 14, 17, 19, 23, 39, 48, 56, 60, 64, 68, 82, 86, 92, 97, 101, 105, 110, 112, 125, 126, 130, 137, 143, 145, 149, 152, 157, 163, 175

sum, 3, 11, 12, 23, 24, 30, 41, 47, 49, 55, 56, 58, 59, 60, 61, 66, 72, 83, 86, 92, 93, 96, 98, 101, 104, 109, 110, 111, 112, 113, 114, 118, 119, 123, 126, 127, 128, 129, 136, 138, 141, 146, 149, 150, 157, 164, 167, 169, 175

surface area, 59

T

term, 104, 113, 117, 121, 141

total surface area, 56

trapezoid, 40, 43, 70, 81, 174

triangle, 2, 6, 32, 76, 91, 97, 102, 103, 113, 129, 161, 165, 166, 172, 176

V

vertex, 56, 59, 138, 143

vertical angles, 70

volume, 74, 77, 143, 147, 165

W

whole number, 74, 77, 78, 126, 145, 146

whole numbers, 74, 77, 78, 146

Y

y-axis, 74

Z

zero, 43, 67, 83, 126, 130, 131

Made in the USA
Las Vegas, NV
25 February 2024